HURON COUNTY PUBLIC LIBRARY

S0-BQY-036

HURON COUNTY LIBRARY
3 6492 00464598 9

51063

386   Beaton, H.
.50924   From the
Beato   wheelhouse.

                                              895

| BC 4 89 | | |
| JUL 6 '89 40604 | | |

51063

386   Beaton, Horace Louden, 1903-
.50924   From the wheelhouse; the story of a
Beato   Great Lakes captain [by] Horace L. Beaton
             [and] Charles P. Beaton. Cheltenham, Ont.,
             Boston Mills Press, 1979.
                79 p. illus., maps.

             1. Beaton, Horace Louden, 1903-
             2. Shipmasters - Ontario - Biography.
             3. Great Lakes - Navigation - History.
             I. Beaton, Charles P., 1935-   II. Title.
             091982224X pb   0933805

                                          6/HE/CN

From The Wheelhouse
The Story of A Great Lakes Captain

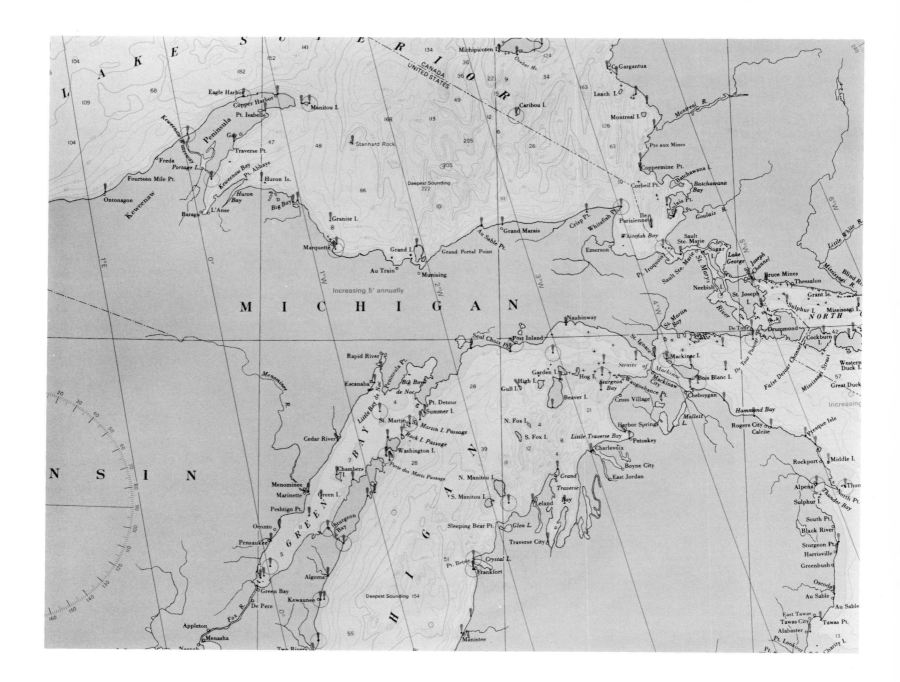

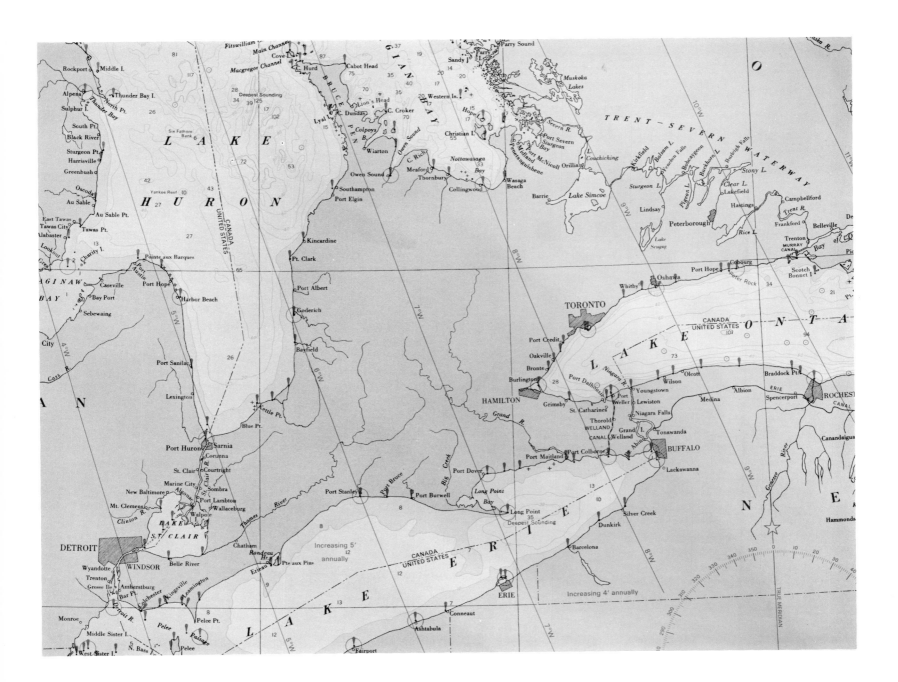

From The Wheelhouse
The Story of A Great Lakes Captain
ISBN 0-919822-24-X
Copyright © Horace L. Beaton, Charles P. Beaton, 1979.

Published in Canada by
THE BOSTON MILLS PRESS
R.R. 1 CHELTENHAM, ONTARIO
LOP ICO

We gratefully acknowledge the assistance of The Canada Council and The Ontario Arts Council in the publishing of this book.

FROM THE WHEELHOUSE

The Story of A Great Lakes Captain

51063

JAN 17 '80

HORACE L. BEATON   CHARLES P. BEATON

THE BOSTON 1979 MILLS PRESS

Prologue

My father has always been a great storyteller, and the stories are best told when he is with other Great Lakes sailors. In such company, the drama and the humour of life on the ships is revealed in the most colourful language you can imagine.

My children, now teenagers, have been fascinated with their Grandfather Beaton. They are too young to remember most of the ships, but they liked his stories. Whenever the family got together, they would often ask, "Grandpa, tell us about the time . . .", and the captain would tell another familiar story, just the way he had told it many times before with all the appropriate dramatic action.

Gradually, it dawned on me that we were sharing in a living history of a very special part of Canada. The Great Lakes system is a unique chain of fresh water which allows shipping to and from the heart of the North American continent. The lakes have their own history — of early sailing days, shipwrecks, passenger boats, and giant ore and grain carriers. A lot has been written about the lore of the lakes and various shipping disasters, but little has been written by the men who sailed the Great Lakes ships. Why was that? Perhaps they didn't think of their jobs as all that important. Most of them regarded work on the ships as just another job. Their jobs, however, involved some danger and a great deal of skill.

My father's career began in one era and ended in another. He can remember old captains who could run certain parts of Georgian Bay in a thick fog without any navigation aids, and tell how far off shore they were by the smell of the cedar trees. He retired as master of a new fast ship with all the electronic navigation aids and diesel engines controlled directly from the wheelhouse. It was a ship that could almost run itself.

My attempts to gather my dad's stories by using a tape recorder and rewriting them met with frustration. Dad was intimidated by "that gadget" and I couldn't get him to talk into it with any sense of continuity. So, I asked him to write down all of the ships on which he sailed, and make note of any interesting events he could remember. Dad did so well on this that he filled two school scribblers, top to bottom, front to back. What follows is his story, just the way he wrote it, with some minor editing on grammar and the formulation of paragraphs and chapters.

The stories are recorded mainly for my children, Mark, Kathryn and Miriam Beaton; and my sister's children, Brian, Bruce and Lynne Sweeney. Sometime in the future, either they or their children may appreciate that there was a Great Lakes captain in their heritage. This little book will help them know something about his life, work and the ships he sailed.

I want to thank several people who helped in producing this book. Mrs. Jennifer Barr, friend and author, initially encouraged me to get the story into a book and directed me to the publishers. My brother-in-law, Mr. John Weichel, managing editor of the Stratford Beacon Herald, gave valuable direction to the text. Mrs. Valerie Johnston, my secretary, did valiantly in the translation and typing of the manuscript. My sister, Joan (Mrs. Graham Sweeney of Sarnia), and my wife, Jean, added the necessary encouragement to Dad and myself to get it all together.

I trust that "From the Wheelhouse, The Story of a Great Lakes Captain" will be interesting and enjoyable for all who read it.

Rev. Charles P. Beaton, B.A., B.D.
Trinity United Church,
Acton, Ontario
April, 1979.

*This book is dedicated
to
Marjorie Evelyn Tobey Beaton
whose love and faithfulness
sustained us all.*

Yonge St., Tara, 1896

1
CHAPTER

The Beginnings

I was born March 1, 1903, in the village of Tara, Arran Township, Bruce County, Ontario, and named Horace Louden Beaton, son of John Beaton and Mary Ann Forrest. John Beaton was a harness maker in Tara. He was born in Edinburgh, Scotland in 1850 or 1851, but there is no record of his birth. In an old family Bible, there is a record of marriage in St. Cuthbert's Parish, Edinburgh, Scotland, of Lewis Hilliard Beaton and Elizabeth Clazey in 1849.

The two sons, John and James, born to them were only one and two years old when the family emigrated to United States. Lewis Beaton was a stonemason and was killed when he fell off a building on which he was working, about a year after coming to Brooklyn, New York. William C. Henderson, a partner of Lewis Beaton, married the widow, Elizabeth, and took up a homestead in Derby Township, Grey County, near Keady, Ontario.

My mother, Mary Ann Forrest, was born on a farm in Sullivan Township on the east side of the county line between Grey and Bruce Counties. Her father, Robert Forrest, and her mother, Esther Bingham, were of Irish descent. I am told that my grandmother Esther was born on a sailing ship crossing the Atlantic.

Mary Ann Forrest, always known as "Minnie", was married to John Beaton in 1889 in Wiarton, Ontario. They had three sons — Lewis, born in 1890, who later moved to Waterloo, Iowa, U.S.A.; Percy, born in 1891, enlisted in the army in 1914 in Winnipeg and died of wounds March 16, 1918, in France in the Great War.

I was an "afterthought", coming along twleve years later, but my boyhood days in Tara were delightful. I haunted the Sauble River that ran through the village and was either on, at, or in it most of the time. In the spring, I would hunt muskrats and fish for pike. Fish were plentiful in those days. I built rafts and sailed down the river with the current, guided by a long pole. In the summer, I swam in several swimming holes every day. When winter came, I skated on every part of the river, up to Arranville and down to Allenford. Sometimes, I was on it before the ice was thick enough to hold, which resulted in breaking through and getting soaking wet. Then, I would head home fast, with my wet clothes freezing stiff before I got there. My mother always said I turned her hair grey much sooner than it should have.

During the summer when I was fifteen, I worked for Duff Brothers Apiary. They had several "bee yards" and extracted the honey in the Tara plant. When school started in the fall, I kept on working for them until we had all the "bees" laid up for the winter. I then drove a rural mail route for Joe Grant. He had three rural mail routes out of Tara Post Office. My mother had begged me to go back to school, as there was a high school in Tara. But, I decided I would not return to school, and I had to think of a job somewhere.

YONGE ST. TARA

1896

So, in April, 1919, with about $18 in my pocket, I took the train to Midland, Ontario. I knew a couple of chaps who had already left Tara to go sailing on the Great Lakes and they had gone to Midland to get their ships. I arrived in Midland and I never saw more ships in my life. The harbour was full, but I found I was too early to get a job as deck hand. Only the engineer crews were working, fitting out the engines. The Great War was now over, but the men from the army had not arrived

home in Canada, as yet. There were lots of jobs available. Every ship wanted to hire me as a fireman. I didn't want to shovel coal, so I kept on looking.

The railroad station was right on the harbour waterfront and I was standing on the station platform when the passenger train pulled in. I happened to get talking to a chap who said he was going to look for a job as a fireman. He pointed to a small white ship tied up not far from the station. He said he had gone over there and the mate had offered him a deck-hand's job, but he did not want it. I told him I had just been on a ship that wanted a fireman, so he headed for that ship and I headed for the white ship. The mate hired me right away.

This ship was the Canadian Government Ship (C.G.S.) "Lambton" and was working out of the Government Marine Agency in Parry Sound. Their work was maintaining aids to navigation and taking supplies to lighthouses. We would put all spar buoys in the narrow channels and paint range lights. This was interesting work to me, a sixteen-year-old. We went around all the channels and lighthouses around Georgian Bay. The ship would go in as far as it could, then anchor. We would then lower our power boat and work boat, load them with spar buoys and concrete anchors. Then, towing the work boat with the power boat, we would go up the channel to the Port Severn Lock. The ice would take some of the spar buoys out of position These we would put back into position and paint them. If the buoy was missing, we would put a new one in place with a concrete anchor. Key Harbour was another channel that had a lot of spar buoys to paint and put in place. In midsummer, we took supplies of drums of kerosene and all necessary supplies to the lighthouses at Cape Croker, Flower Pot Island, and Cove Island, to mention a few.

The Lambton was all white hull and deck houses and it had to be kept spotless. We used to scrub the whitework with "soogee", made with soap and lye and boiled with a steam pipe. I remember the ends of my fingers being raw and bleeding plenty of times. The painting was better, as you didn't have your hands in hot lye soogee. The ship was always kept in tiptop shape.

In running on the open water, the wheelsman had to steer the ship. I envied him, standing behind the wheel, steering a compass course. One wheelsman, Fred Baker from Bayfield, Ontario, would let me steer the ship when we had no other work to do. He was glad to show me how to keep the ship on course. This ship had a dake steam gear right in the wheelhouse. You didn't have to turn the wheel a full

C. G. S. LAMBTON
LOST ON LAKE SUPERIOR
APRIL 1922

C.G.S. LAMBTON

turn. Just move the wheel right or left enough to open the valve, the steam gear would run until you shut it off. That would turn the drum with the chain around it and move the rudder the required amount. This ship had twin screw propellors and it was no easy job to keep on course. When Fred Baker quit in October of 1919, they gave me the job of wheelsman. We finished the season and laid up in Midland. The captain was John Brown from Owen Sound and first mate Mitchell from Orillia. I must have worked to suit them as they gave me a job on the Lambton again for the spring of 1920.

Our work was the same routine, with aids to navigation and supplies to lighthouses. This routine was changed in the summer of 1920, as the Lambton was dispatched to Amherstburg, Ontario. A new concrete base was being built around Colchester Lighthouse on Lake Erie. A government engineer from Ottawa was laying out the work for the contractor and he was to live aboard the Lambton. The Lambton would leave Amherstburg every morning and run down to Colchester Lighthouse. The crew would launch a boat and row over to the light-house with the government engineer. While he was busy with the contractor, I would go up to the top of the lighthouse. The light-keeper had a telescope and I could sit there and try and read the names of the ships that were always going or coming past the lighthouse. In those years, the sidewheel passenger ships were very busy running between Detroit, Buffalo and Cleveland. These ships were nice to watch. They were fast and you could hear the flop-flop of their paddle wheels for miles.

I quit the Lambton at Amherstburg in October of 1920 and went back home to Tara. I had no good reason, only I decided I would not follow the ships anymore. It may have been fate, as this ship was later to meet a tragic end. In the spring of 1922, the Lambton left Sault Ste. Marie to take the light-keeper and his wife to Caribou Island on Lake Superior. Apparently, the Lambton was stuck in the ice in Whitefish Bay for several hours. She eventually cleared the ice, rounded the light at Whitefish Point, and that was the last seen of her. The Lambton never reached Caribou Island and disappeared with all hands. Several of the crew that I had worked with were still on her. I was in Regina, Saskatchewan, in the spring of 1922 when I read about its disappearance. My thoughts went back to October 1920 and I wondered what made me leave this ship.

I drove the rural mail route again and in April, 1921, I went to western Canada with two friends, Henry and Bob Berry. I got a job as a mechanic's helper in a garage in Regina. This lasted till the end of December when winter closed up all car driving. I stayed in Regina for the month of January and I walked all over the city looking for a job. I am sure there were 10,000 others doing the same thing. No jobs available and no money left, I decided to go to my brother's home in Wapella, Saskatchewan. I had been boarding with an aunt and uncle in Regina. They were real good to me and I had my board paid up to the end of January and had only about $5 left to buy a railroad ticket to Wapella. I told my brother I was broke and no job until next spring when automobiles started running again. He and his wife, Bessie, had three kids to keep, but said I better stay with them until spring. Lew bought me a season ticket at the skating rink, so I was able to skate and play hockey with the Wapella hockey team. Spring came at last and, my mother having sent me some money, I returned to Regina and worked in the garage again. I made up my mind that I would not be caught in western Canada another winter and planned to go to the harvest fields in August. I was lucky in meeting up with a cousin of my mother's who was in Regina to visit the exhibition. I talked to him about getting a job in the harvest. He said if I would like to go back to Ogema, Saskatchewan, south of Regina, with him, he would give me a job in a week's time when he started to cut his grain.

I worked for George Koehler from August until November on his farm. My job was to fire the steam engine for the threshing machine. I got up at 4:00 a.m. and walked about three-quarters of a mile, started up the fire and had steam when the crew came out to work. I then walked back and had breakfast. The engineer and separator man kept the engine fired up until I got there. If the dew didn't come down too heavy or too soon, we were able to thresh until 9:00 p.m. It was a long day, but the money was good and your board went with it. On November fourth, I got up as usual at 4:00 a.m. and stepped out into about three or four inches of snow. I went back into the bunk house and went to bed. There would by no threshing with snow on the ground. After breakfast, I told George I would be leaving and heading back east. He said we would be threshing again when it dried up, but I decided I wouldn't wait. I now had a nice nest egg so left Ogema for Regina, picked up the rest of my belongings and took the train to Wapella. I told my brother I had only come this time for a visit before going home. My brother said he had been talking with a chap from Tara who had come out on the harvest excursion and was going to stay and work out there. The thought came to me if he came out there on the harvest excursion, he should have a return half of his ticket and, if he was not going back, it would be no good to him. I got in touch with him on the telephone and he said he sure had the return half of his ticket and would be in town Saturday night, two days away. He came in and I gave him $5 for the return ticket to Tara, Ontario. So, I was lucky to get right home on that ticket and also save some money. I hung around Tara that winter skating, playing hockey and driving a rural mail route again, once in a while. I decided I would go back to the lakes again, this time in the bigger cargo ships.

Yonge St., Tara, 1930

MIDLAND PRINCE

2
CHAPTER

Back to the Lakes

I went to Owen Sound and looked up mates whose addresses I had and was given a job as wheelsman on S.S. Midland Prince. The Prince was owned by Canada Steamship Lines and was about 500 feet long, a straight deck type with about 14 or 15 hatches. These hatches were wooden covers and were covered by tarpaulins. All had to be handled manually. This ship carried grain, coal and iron ore. Cargoes of iron ore were unloaded at Point Edward at that time. Whirleys would unload into ore cars on C.N.R. track, which were transported to the Steel Company in Hamilton. This was before the present Welland Canal was built. Today, much larger ships transit the Welland Canal with much bigger cargoes. I spent all season of 1923 on the Midland Prince. We unloaded ore at Point Edward, just ahead of the Northern Navigation dock. The three passenger boats, Noronic, Hamonic and Huronic, used this dock to load passengers and package freight. I always admired these ships, beautifully painted with black hulls, white super structure and red, white and black smoke stacks, the colours of Canada Steamship Lines. The Northern Navigation Co. was a division of C.S.L. If we were at the ore dock unloading on the day one of these ships was scheduled to leave, I would watch longingly, for I was fascinated by the hustle and bustle which surrounded them. Buses returned passengers who had been on a picnic to Lake Huron Beach. Then, the C.N.R. boat train from Toronto would pull up to the ship's side. At 4 p.m., the ship scheduled to leave on that day would slide away from the dock. Passengers would be throwing money off the ship into the water of the St. Clair River where the kids, shivering and waiting, would dive for it. They would battle to see who could come up with the coin. The water was so clear, you could see the coin wobbling its way down. The lucky diver would put the coin in his mouth, as it was the only way to hold it. Some of them had quite a cheekful by the time the boat pulled out.

I admired the Hamonic most of all. Often, when I was on watch on the Midland Prince, she would pass us at night, lights blazing, and soon by out of sight ahead. On a clear night, her rakish lines and all lights glittering on the water, the Hamonic was a picture to behold. It was a thrill to see this ship running under full power, and I set my heart on getting a job on her. The first mate of the Midland Prince was a friend of Andy Allen, the first mate of the Hamonic. When I finished the season on the Midland Prince, I wrote to Andy for a wheeling job on the Hamonic, enclosing a recommendation from the mate of Midland

Prince. I got the job. Little did I know then that this ship would be a very important part of my sailing career.

In late March of 1924, I got word to report for fitout of the Hamonic in Sarnia. I soon found out why the passenger boats always looked so clean and smart. We started in to soogee and scrub all the white superstructure. Then, we painted everything from the top of those tall masts to the waterline.

I liked the job wheeling in the Hamonic. There were four wheelsmen at that time and watches were six-hour shifts. You put in three hours at the wheel and three hours as lookout. About midsummer, there was an opening for a third mate. This job required no certificate, as you had no watch to stand. But, you had eight deckhands handling winches and lines to tie up and all other jobs in maintaining the ship in spic and span condition. I finished the season of 1924 in this position and decided I would go after a mate's certificate during the winter.

I enrolled in the Toronto Nautical School and started instruction in January, 1925. By mid-March, I was ready to take the examination before the government examiner for first mate's certificate. This exam took a couple of days and I was successful in passing. The captain of the Midland Prince, whom I had wheeled for in 1923, gave me the job of second mate of the Midland Prince. Out of the passenger boats and back into bulk cargo ships again. This 1925 season was slow for cargoes and the Midland Prince tied up in Fort William and paid off the crew. It so happened the Hamonic came in that day and was docked at the C.P.R. shed just ahead of where we tied up the Midland Prince. I went over to the Hamonic to see some of my old shipmates. The first mate said they needed a wheelsman, would I come? I was only too glad of a job, so back on the passenger boats again. I was there about two months when the Midland Prince was notified to start out again. I put in the rest of the season as second mate on the Midland Prince.

While I was wheeling on the Hamonic, Capt. Johnston from Port Dalhousie had been captain on the Hamonic, relieving Capt. Montgomery. I knew he was captain of the Sarnian, a C.S.L. ten-hatch cargo boat. This ship was smaller than the Midland Prince and it seemed to me was having a better time securing cargoes, with less time laying up. I thought it better to get in a full season's work. Knowing that Capt. Johnston wanted a second mate, I wrote him during the winter and secured the second mate's job on S.S. Sarnian. We started the 1926 season out of Goderich and the ice was so bad this spring, it was May before we got going. We only got a mile or two outside Goderich and were stuck in the ice for three or four days.

We were backing up and going ahead in this hard ice. The big chunks of hard ice were piling up around our propellor. Finally, we broke off two of the propeller blades. These blades were cast iron. Four individual blades bolted to a hub fitted on the tail shaft. We were very near helpless in the ice with only two blades on the propellor. After three or four days, the wind changed and it loosened up the ice so we were able to turn around and go back into Goderich harbour. We pumped all the ballast water from after tanks and filled all ballast tanks forward, also water into number one cargo hold, we were able to tip the propeller hub out of water. The engineers took off the stubs of the old blades and we took two of our spare blades that were stowed on deck. With our mooring winches and mooring cables, we were able to hoist the spare blades over the ship's side and pull them back and over the hub. We lowered them into place and the engineers bolted on the two new blades. We then proceeded out of Goderich and headed for the Lakehead with no further trouble.

After several loads of grain, we were sent to North Shore Lake Superior to load pulpwood. This was a new cargo for me. We anchored the Sarnian in a bay in the Moffat Straits between St. Ignace and Simpson Island. This is near the entrance to Nipigon Bay. It was beautiful scenery, the land being high and wooded. The green trees came right down to the water's edge. In June, the evenings were long and we could sit out on deck and enjoy the lovely fresh air. Also, on these evenings, we could count five or six moose standing in the water by the shore. They could put their heads under water for such a long time. All you could see was the top of their backs and then, with a spray of water, the big rack of horns would come up above the surface. They would chew all the while, take on another lungful of air and go down again. Since it took four or five days to take on a load of pulpwood, we had time to row a lifeboat ashore where we could usually find a small stream and fish for speckled trout. One day, we worked our way up the stream. At the top, there was a little lake with a beaver dam where the lake emptied into the small stream. On the shore a short distance away, two deer were grazing, paying no attention to us. Further along the shore of the lake stood a huge moose with a rack of horns wider than I could stretch my arms. The scene was so beautiful, we just stood and tried to take in all of it. Then, with a shout and a wave of our arms, the moose took off through the bush. The deer raised their heads, took a look at us and went on feeding.

Our first load of pulpwood was an experience for all of us. A small

S.S. HAMONIC arriving at Sarnia, Ontario (photo courtesy of Paisley Collection, Sarnia)

S.S. SARNIAN — Before being changed to C.S.L. colours (photo courtesy of Ron Beaupre)

tug pulled a jack-ladder out to the anchored ship. It was tied up alongside and could be moved to load each hatch. Then the tug towed a raft of pulpwood out to the ship. When this raft was secured alongside, the wood was fed to the jack-ladder. The jack-ladder had a conveyor belt with spikes which took the pulpwood sticks up and dumped them into the cargo hold. When all holds were full, the wood was piled on top of hatches. This was the first load of pulpwood the first mate had anything to do with. It was his job to see that this pulpwood was loaded right and to take on as much as possible. A crew of lumberjacks, armed with picaroons, an instrument that looked like an axe handle with a spike pick on one end, would straighten out and pile this wood in the cargo holds and on deck. The mate was watching the draft marks and, as the wood kept piling up higher and higher, the weight had not put the ship down to the draft we could load to. Then, all of a sudden, the ship took a list to starboard, the first mate waved his arms and shouted, "Shut it off". Too late, the load was too high and made the ship unstable. We started water ballast into the tanks on high side and, when the ship was about even keel, it would list the other way.

We ended up filling the ballast tanks both sides. With a small list, we headed out on Lake Superior for Sault Ste Marie and carried the list all the way to Erie, Pennsylvania, where the pulpwood was unloaded. We were locked down in the American locks at Sault Ste. Marie. As the water in the lock was let out and the ship was going down in the lock, the steel cables tying the ship to the lock wall were too tight and the more the ship went down, the more it would list over. It had enough list that the pulpwood logs piled on deck slid off the low side into the water in the lock. The lock master was mad and had us tie the ship up below the lock to see if we could get the ship back on even keel. By pumping some water ballast, we were able to straighten up nearly even keel, but we still had a list until we unloaded.

The season of 1926 was a little slow for the ships to get cargoes and the Sarnian was laid up in August. The crew were paid off and I went home to Tara. I had only been home a week when I got a call to go to the Hamonic as second mate. This was my old love. I was happy to get the job and finished the season there.

The winter of 1926-27 was spent in Tara and I had a letter from Capt. Montgomery, who was the captain of the Hamonic; he was going on a bulk cargo boat, the S.S. Osler. He wanted me to go with him as first mate. This was a step up the ladder and I accepted. This ship was in the coal, grain and iron-ore trade. The Osler was busy into September and again, cargoes were scarce and the ship was tied up in Fort William. The ship had to go to dry-dock for her five-year inspection but, as the dry-dock was busy, they had to wait until it was clear. Again, the crew were paid off and I was back home in Tara. I had been home only a short time when I read that the M.V. Alice had run on the rocks at Cape Chin, north of Lion's Head. This ship was owned by John Tackaberry from Lion's head and had a run carrying cargo and passengers from Owen Sound, Lion's head, Tobermory, Southbay Mouth and Providence Bay on Manitoulin Island. The Alice had been a quarantine tug on the east coast. Her work was to take inspectors out to foreign ships anchored in quarantine before they were cleared to come into their berths at dockside. The Alice was a steel hull with twin steam engines. This was a strongly-built hull and she had equipment on board to fumigate the foreign ship in quarantine if necessary.

John Tackaberry bought this tug and brought her up to Owen Sound where the steam engines were removed and twin diesel engines installed. He raised the deck house and built a deck with cabins. This was above the original deck on the Alice, which became a "tween" deck

to carry cargo and automobiles. Tackaberry had the franchise to carry automobiles from Tobermory to South Bay on Manitoulin Island, a short route from Toronto to the Soo. They made two trips a week at this time and the cars were loaded and unloaded on the opposite side of the harbour from the present dock in Tobermory. The Alice could only take about eight to ten cars. Several ships had been on this run before, but they were smaller. The automobile traffic was increasing and the Alice was a big improvement.

After reading of the Alice running ashore and that she was back in Owen Sound, I wondered if they would need a new crew. So, I went to Owen Sound and looked up Mr. Tackaberry and inquired about a job. He was getting a new captain and had already hired a first mate. Until this time, he had only employed a captain and mate and they had to do their own wheeling on their watch. He thought that this was too much for a mate to be tying up, loading cargo and then have to stand a watch and do the steering. He had decided to hire a second mate and I could have the job. Harry McCoy from Manitouwaning was first mate, so he and I stood watch and watch, doing our own wheeling. This worked very well as we could get some rest when being off watch.

On the last trip of the season, the Alice was to go to Lion's Head and load bagged peas for Owen Sound. The farmers brought wagon loads of peas to the dock and we loaded them aboard ship. It was hard work and took all day and well into the evening. When the Alice sailed out of the bay and hauled around the point headed east, for Cape Croker, there was a strong north-east wind. She listed badly over to starboard and stayed there. There was very little sea running, but I didn't like the list, so I "hightailed" it down to the deckhands' room. They were all tired and in their bunks. I dragged them all out and told them if they didn't want a swim in cold Georgian Bay, that they better get down on deck and start moving bags of peas. The list of the boat was enough to get them moving. We piled bags of peas on the high side of the deck and took most of the list out of the boat; we made it into Owen Sound with only a slight list. I was sure glad to get to the dock and see that load off the boat.

A few years later, the Owen Sound Transportation Co. bought the Alice and she was renamed Hibou. She continued to carry passengers and freight for her new owners out of Owen Sound. One night, after loading freight, the Hibou departed Owen Sound and, while still in Owen Sound Bay, she rolled over and sank with the loss of some lives. Captain Norman Mackay was one of those lost in this accident.

HIBOU formerly ALICE

In spring of 1928, I heard that they wanted a first mate for S.S. Thousand Islander, a small passenger boat, built as a day pleasure boat to carry sight-seers through the Thousand Islands. She was 173 feet long and had a shallow draft of about ten feet and would carry 875 passengers on a day trip only, no overnight accomodation for passengers. The Canada Steamship Lines brought this ship up from lower lakes to run from Windsor and Detroit every day in summer months. One day, she would leave Windsor-Detroit for a run across Lake st. Clair, up St. Clair River to the entrance to Snye Carte, then up the winding river to Wallaceburg. The next day, she would leave Windsor and Detroit and run across Lake St. Clair to the entrance of Thames River, then up the Thames River to Chatham, Ontario. Being shallow draft, she could navigate the winding Thames. The Thousand Islander had twin screws. We could back up on one engine and go ahead

on the other, with the help of the steering rudder to make some of the turns. She also carried charter parties out of Chatham for a day's outing on Belle Isle, Detroit, a great picnic summer resort. This run was a nice day's outing in hot summer days and passengers could take along their own picnic baskets or the ship had a good cafeteria to serve them. We also took out moonlight cruises some evenings each week.

One incident occurred on a fourth of July holiday. This day, we had a full load to Chatham and back. There was to be a moonlight cruise that evening out of Detroit. We landed at our dock at the foot of Brush Street and the dock was full of passengers for the moonlight cruise. About 875 passengers were still aboard and the moonlight cruise passengers waiting to get on, made quite a crowd of people. The passengers on board all crowded to the side coming to the dock and gave the ship a list to the dock side. We had just finished tying up when a

Steamer THOUSAND ISLANDER on Sydenham River near Wallaceburg, Ontario circa 1921 (photo courtesy of Mann Historical Files)

man on the dock, whom I didn't know, hollered up, "Mate, those lower portholes are open and under water". I made a bee line through the crowd for the engine room. I found the chief engineer and oiler looking over the crowd on dock. I could hear the water pouring into lower engine room from open portholes. When I told the engineer about it and he could then hear the water coming in, there was some fast moving by the three of us for lower engine room. We had a job getting those portholes closed against the pressure of the water, and we have an unknown man to thank for giving us the warning about the portholes being open. It wouldn't have taken very long the way the water was pouring in, to have been in real trouble. The Thousand Islander could have rolled over and sank at the dock.

With automobiles coming into their own and the picnic passengers getting fewer, the company discontinued these summer trips in August, 1928. We were ordered back up to Sarnia to lay up. A short time later, the Thousand Islander was sold to Georgian Bay interests. The S.S. Collingwood, bound for Midland with a load of coal, was to tow the Thousand Islander to Midland to her new owners. The Collingwood started out with the tow in the fall and ran into bad weather crossing Saginaw Bay. The Thousand Islander, being built more for river work, soon found that the heavy pounding she was taking was too much for her. The steel hawser tow line was pulling the front end of the ship apart. The Collingwood was able to get alongside the Thousand Islander and take off the skeleton crew she had aboard. The Thousand Islander sank shortly after with no loss of life.

I had gone home to Tara and about a week later, I had a call to see if I would go second mate on the S.S. Renvoyle, a package freighter which was being put on the Point Edward-Lakehead freight run. The passenger ship, Huronic, had run aground between Port Arthur and Duluth and the Renvoyle was to take her freight. I made two and a half trips on her as second mate. On the third trip, we arrived at Lakehead; the District Manager for C.S.L. came down to the ship while we were unloading at C.P.R. sheds in Fort William. He told me I was to go to the Huronic in Port Arthur dry dock. The "Huey" had been taken off the rocks, repaired and was ready to come off the dry dock the next day to resume her scheduled passenger run. I was to be first mate and a Capt. Brown from one of the bulk freight boats was to be the new captain.

The passenger run was not new to me, as I had been on the Hamonic in 1924 and 1926. Capt. Brown had never been on a passenger run before and was in the habit of using some rough language at times.

He knew the passengers could overhear some of his language and once he said to me, "God, Horace, I'll have to be more careful the way I talk on this ship." About the first trip we had into Duluth, we were backing away from the dock into the harbour to turn and head for the lift bridge at the entrance to Duluth Harbour from Lake Superior. One of the American ore carriers was also coming down the harbour, heading for the bridge. Capt. Brown was going astern and it looked as if we were backing across in front of the big ore carrier. The American ship blew a danger signal and Capt. Brown put the Huronic ahead and moved out of his road. The ore carrier then passed very close to the Huronic, and the captain on the ore carrier came out of the wheelhouse and yelled something. I was still standing on bow deck and Capt. Brown up in the wheelhouse of Huronic, could hear this captain of the ore boat yelling, but couldn't make out what he said. He stuck his head out the front window that was open and said to me, "What did he say, mate? What did he say?" So, I looked up and said, "He just asked if you thought you were handling a threshing machine!". Well, that was just like waving a red flag in a bull ring. Brown ran out of the wheelhouse onto the wing of the bridge, shaking his fist at the passing ore boat. The air turned blue and, by this time, all the passengers out on deck watching our departure were looking up in wonder and amazement. Capt. Brown only made a few trips on the Huronic after this and then went back to his own ship in the bulk freight run. Capt. T.S. Patterson, the former captain of the Huronic came back and finished the season of 1928.

I continued as first mate of the Huronic for the next three years. Then, in 1932, Capt. Patterson was moving to the Renvoyle and asked me to go with him. While I was first mate of the Renvoyle, I remember an incident that happened. We had been tied up at C.P.R. sheds in the Kam River, Fort William east. After unloading package freight at C.P.R. sheds, sometimes the captain would remain there the rest of the night before moving to a loading dock. We were booked to load newsprint paper at Great Lakes Paper Mill. This mill is located on the Kaministiqua River as far up as the ships can go. This particular trip, we were to start loading at the Great Lakes dock at 8:00 a.m. Capt. T.S. Patterson decided we would stay tied up at C.P.R. shed all night and leave early the next morning. It takes about an hour to make the run from C.P.R. sheds to Great Lakes dock and we pass through two bridges on the way. At 6:15 in the morning, I had all the crew up and standing by to let go and leave to go up the river. I called the captain and was standing by waiting for him to signal "let go". We waited and waited

HURONIC on rocks Lucille Island, Lake Superior 1928

RENVOYLE

and no signal to let go. I went and looked through the port hole to the captain's bed room. He was still fast asleep. So, I went in and said, "Captain, it will keep us jumping to get to the paper mill in time to start loading." He jumped up and told me to go to wheelhouse and let go and proceed up the river. This was done and we were through the bridge at Ogilvie's elevator when the captain came up. The Renvoyle was moving right along at full speed. We went around a couple of bends and started to approach the second bridge. This bridge is a swing bridge, turning on a center turntable. It is located right near Patterson's elevator and is the main route out of Fort William for Duluth. Capt. Patterson blew the whistle signal to open the bridge. There was no response or no movement of the bridge. The captain blew the whistle the second time, the Renvoyle still going full speed. Just then a street car came up the track and onto the bridge to cross. The captain said, "I guess I better check down; it don't look as if they are going to open up." I was standing looking out the front wheelhouse window and I could feel my hair starting to stand up on my head. The street car crossed and was off the bridge on the opposite side and a man ran onto the bridge and went up the ladder to the control tower. By now, the captain had the engines going full astern. Patterson, who was always cool in a crisis said "Horace, it looks like we are going to hit that bridge." And we did! — CRASH — the bridge rocked up on the center turntable and I was sure it was going to crash right over, but by now, the ship was going astern and the bridge dropped back into position. We had put a six-foot deep "v" in the steel beams of the bridge. I was standing at the back of the wheelhouse, frozen in shock. The captain, not the least bit excited, told me to get the lines ready to tie up at Patterson elevator dock. Before we got tied up, the bridge swung open and we proceeded through and went on to tie up at the Great Lakes Paper dock, only about twenty minutes late.

We were to be on the Point Edward to the Lakehead package freight run and, at the end of the season after we laid up, I continued as watchman for the winter. My duties were to sound the ballast tanks to make sure no water was coming in, check mooring lines and make sure everything was in order aboard a laid-up ship. I was alone and doing my own housekeeping. Alongside were two laid-up ships and Bill and Verna Fraser were the ship keepers. So, I had some company close by to help put in time. I had decided to do this shipkeeping to help save up some money, as I was planning to get married at the end of 1933 season. The chief engineer and his crew came aboard the first of April to fitout

the boilers and engine room. I left when they arrived and went home to Tara to have a week or so holiday before starting out on the Renvoyle for another season. I expected to be called to the Renvoyle about April 15, and had a crew standing by. I kept waiting for the call to come until nearly May and I got a little anxious when I didn't hear anything. Finally, I called the captain at his home in Toronto. He said, "I was just going to call you to tell you that the engine room crew had been paid off and that the Renvoyle was not going to run this season. The package freight was light and the other two ships were going to handle it." The hungry thirties had started for me, planning to get married and no job. All the crew I had standing by had to be notified that they had no jobs.

By May 1, 1933, all the ships that were going to run had started and no jobs were available. I began to assess my chances of getting a job of any kind. I knew the passenger boat S.S. Manitoulin, owned by Owen Sound Transportation Co., was tied up in Owen Sound. This ship carried freight and passengers from Owen Sound, up the "Turkey Trail" as it was known to most sailors. The summer schedule started about July 1 to the middle of September. The route was from Owen Sound, calling at Killarney, Manitowaning, Little Current, Kagawong, Gore Bay, Blind River, Thessalon, Hilton Beach, Richards Landing and Sault Ste. Marie. From the Soo, they made a side trip down St. Mary's River to Mackinac Island, a lovely American summer resort, and stayed overnight. They then returned to the Soo and made the same calls on the return to Owen Sound. This was a real nice trip. The scenery was grand and the passengers liked this trip very much.

On one trip down-bound, we had cattle to load at Kagawong. Ossie Long, the first mate, and I were trying to get those steers to go up the gangplank and on to the ship. We were having some trouble with some of them. They would balk at the gangplank and we would have to prod and twist their tails and do most everything to get them on board. Tim Lodge, the wheelsman, was standing inside the gangway door on the "tween" deck as these cattle came through. One of the more obstinate steers was giving the mate and I trouble getting him up the gangplank. All of a sudden, he lowered his head and gave a snort and went through the gangway on the run. As he landed on deck, he swung his dirty tail, catching Lodge right across the mouth. He had on a white shirt and tie and the white collar was a mess. Ossie Long and I laughed so much we nearly split our sides. Lodge was so mad, he found a two by four and we had to forcibly stop him from killing that steer. We put these cattle in pens of hardwood planks, bolted up tight to keep the cattle from

MANITOULIN

moving or even lying down. This was July and the weather being warm, we always had a big job cleaning up our freight deck after unloading the cattle in Owen Sound.

I was with the Manitoulin all summer and, when the last scheduled trip in September was over, we were lucky to have an added trip of interest to all of us. The World's Fair was on in Chicago, and the Owen Sound Transportation Co. arranged a trip on the Manitoulin to the World's Fair at Chicago. About a hundred passengers were aboard and had a good trip across Georgian Bay, Lake Huron and through the Straits of mackinaw and down Lake Michigan. We went right into Chicago and tied up between two bridges in the heart of the city, only about ten minutes from the fair grounds. I feel I was lucky to be able to get to a world's fair, as I expect it to be the only world's fair I will see in my lifetime. We stayed in Chicago four days and our passengers used the Manitoulin to live on and had every day to see all the sights of Chicago. We returned to Owen Sound and then laid up the Manitoulin.

I had only been home a few days when I received word to round up a crew and go to Sarnia and fit out the Renvoyle. They decided to start her out on the package freight run October 1, 1933. We ran until December 14, and, as I had planned to get married on December 16, the captain let me off before the ship was laid up. I made it home to Tara and started on a new course on the sea of matrimony with Marjorie Evelyn Tobey, also of Tara.

I went back as first mate on the Renvoyle in 1934 and 1935, and both of those years the Renvoyle ran the package freight run, Windsor, Sarnia and the Lakehead. Since I had acquired my master's certificate from the Toronto Nautical School in 1929, I began to think I would like to be captain of my own ship. The Canada Steamship Lines usually trained all their masters in the smaller, lower-canal boats. All my experience was from Windsor, west, and I felt I better get down the lower canal to get that experience. I applied to the company and was given the first mate's job on the Edmonton and, in spring of 1936, I went to Levis, Quebec, to join her. I wasas green as grass on this run; everything was new to me. The Edmonton was a package freight carrier and was equipped with booms for handling cargo on and off overside. I had never fitted out a boom and I was lucky the second mate had a good knowledge of what was needed. The captain was "Sliver" Anderson, a real character of those days. I told him I didn't know anything about the lower canal and had never been further east than Lake Erie. I had been into Buffalo and Erie, Pennsylvania, Sandusky and Toledo on the bulk boats, earlier. He told me I would just have to learn the lower canal trade and I'm sure he appreciated my knowledge of the upper lakes, as I knew the Detroit River, St. Clair River and St. Mary's River and could help him there. I got along with him well. The two seasons I was on the Edmonton were real interesting and, not only did I learn something of the lower canals, I had a lot of fun.

Capt. Anderson was always pulling something on the other captains. A short time after I had been on the Edmonton, a man came aboard looking for the captain. I took him to the captain and he asked, "Are you Capt. Roy Anderson?" Capt. Anderson said, "I am, better known as 'Sliver', 125 pounds soaking wet."

Capt. Anderson, having a nickname himself, had a nickname for everyone. Other captains, longshoremen, office staff, he had some name for them. He even had a name for me. After I was captain with a ship of my own, I found out his label for me was "The Home Town Boy". This was made up from the fact I was running in and out of Point Edward, my home town. One winter I was enlisted to teach a group of boy Scouts in Sarnia. These scouts required a "Coast Watchman" badge and a "Pilot's" badge to qualify for "Queen's Scout". Captain Anderson found out somehow that I had been teaching these scouts. One time, I heard him talking to another captain over the radio telephone, ship-to-ship, telling him, "I passed 'The Home Town Boy' going up the lake with his Boy Scout uniform on!" Such were the jokes that Capt. Anderson was pulling off all the time. When he retired and left the ships and lakes, everyone missed him, including me.

I put in 1936 and 1937 seasons on the Edmonton and was looking forward to going back in 1938. In early spring, I received a letter from **Mr. King**, district manager for Canada Steamship Lines in Toronto. He stated in his letter that I was appointed to go first mate on the **S.S. Noronic**. This was going back to Northern Navigation passenger run. The Noronic was the largest of the three passenger boats, being the last built and elegantly furnished — their crack passenger ship. I knew that Alex Fraser, who had been first mate of the Noronic ever since she was built, had died and that left this position open. I also knew that he had never been captain of a ship. Whether this was by his own choice or not, I couldn't say. The Noronic was a short season boat, only running June to September. They gave the first mate a twelve-month job. When the ship was laid up, the first mate looked after inside maintenance such as painting kitchen, crew's quarters, staterooms and all inside work. They also had ship's carpenters making repairs when the ship was laid up.

S.S. EDMONTON, 1939

NORONIC, 1938

I did not like this idea, as I was getting away from lower canal experience and had the feeling that I might never be captain of a ship of my own. I wrote a letter to Mr. King in Toronto and told him I did not want to go first mate of Noronic and I pointed out the fact that I would probably never get a ship to sail myself by taking it. Mr. King came right back at me with a letter to come to see him in his office in Toronto at a specified date and time. I went, as requested. Mr. King had my letter on his desk and said, "What do you mean by making the statement that you might never get to be captain of a boat if you accepted the job as first mate of Noronic? Mr. McClymont, operating manager of Canada Steamship Lines in Montreal, picked you out for this job, since you are one of the senior mates who has experience on this run. Now, go home and write a letter confirming that you will go to the Noronic and I will have Mr. McClymont write you a letter stating you will be given a captain's position when your turn comes up." I did as I was told and went to the Noronic in spring of 1938 as first mate.

Captain Bert Atkin was the master and he was an excellent captain. I gained a lot of experience on handling a ship by being associated with him. I knew most of the crew, but had not sailed with any of them. This was my first time on the Noronic. We started fitting out in April, 1938, and a crew of about thirty to thirty-five started to scrub and clean all the white cabins and superstructure. On a ship the size of the Noronic, this was quite a job and when the scrubbing was done, all that white work had to be painted, and when that was done, the black hull from stem to stern. The decks were all grey and usually painted last. The ship must be all ready for early June to make one or two pre-season cruises before starting on the summer schedule. The regular cruise was from Windsor-Detroit, Sarnia, Sault Ste. Marie, Port Arthur, Fort William, Duluth and return, a seven-day trip. We carried package freight and passengers west and, on the return trip, flour and feed to be unloaded at Point Edward. It was then loaded to rail cars to be distributed all over the province of Ontario and some would go to the east coast for export.

I moved the family to Point Edward in the spring of 1938 and was handy to the boat and shed. In 1939, I was still on the Noronic making the same run. The pre-season cruises before summer schedule and and post-season cruises after summer schedule were always popular with the passengers. Out of Cleveland and Detroit to Mackinac Island, into Georgian Bay to Midland, Ontario, where passengers could visit the popular Martyr's Shrine, not far from Midland. Some pre-season or post-season cruises would go down through the Welland Canal to Toronto, down Lake Ontario and through the Thousand Islands as far as Prescott.

Navigating

In the early days, navigating a ship was much by guess and by God. All you had was a magnetic compass. At times, the compass could go crazy due to heavy weather, magnetic attraction and sometimes from the cargo that was loaded. Steel of any kind would change a magnetic compass. I had been told stories of the captain bringing passengers up to the pilot house and bridge. If the ladies got too close to the compass binnacle, the wheelsman was going crazy trying to keep the ship on course. In those days, ladies wore corsets with steel stays and these would set a magnetic compass going crazy. Today's navigating is much easier and better. With the gyro compasses today, steel or magnetic attraction has no effect on the compass. As our navigation on the lakes is all by dead reckoning, it is much easier to get a bearing off a landmark, either by sight or radar and be able to get our position on the chart. The days of the wooden ship and iron men have gone. Today, with all the new electrical gadgets they have, the navigator of a ship must have the knowledge of an electrical engineer.

The Radio Direction Finder was one of the first electrical instruments put on a ship. Radio direction equipment was installed in most of the main lighthouses. The radio would send out a signal from the lighthouse, a series of dots and dashes. Each lighthouse had its own characteristic signal. The R.D.F. on a ship would pick up this signal. The instrument had a turn table graduated on scale of 360 degrees. You could determine the direction the signal was coming from by turning the turn table until the signal was tuned out entirely. Then read the degrees on the scale. From the heading of the ship's compass and the reading of the signal bearing on the R.D.F., you could determine the direction the signal came from. You could take two or three different bearings from lighthouses, draw these direction lines from each of these lighthouses on the chart; where these lines intersect or cross will be the position of the ship.

The captains of the early wooden ships and magnetic compass days have my respect. I marvel at the way they were able to navigate. Instinct and local knowledge was something these captains had. One instance I remember, I was a passenger on a small boat from Sault Ste. Marie to Owen Sound. This was 1927 if my memory is correct. I had crossed Lake Superior from Fort William to Sault Ste. Marie on the C.P.R. Str. Athabaska. Wanting to go to Owen Sound, which was the closest port to my home, I knew the local boats ran down the Turkey Trail, the route from Soo to Owen Sound via the North Channel. Why this was called the "Turkey Trail" I never did find out. This route was hazardous, narrow channels and rocks galore. I found one of the Owen Sound boats was leaving the same day I arrived at the Soo. I went to buy a ticket and they would not sell me a ticket as the ship was booked full. The crew was loading freight and I happened to see the first mate who I knew quite well. I told him I wanted to book passage to Owen Sound but couldn't because all the rooms were full. He said, "Let's go see the ticket agent." He told the ticket agent to sell me a ticket. He said he and the second mate, who I also knew quite well, had a room with two bunks. As one of them would be on watch while the other was off, only one bunk was necessary for them and I could use the other one in their room. This was okay with the ticket agent so I got my ticket and moved aboard. We left the Soo late afternoon and the next morning I had my breakfast and I knew the second mate was on watch and I went up to the wheelhouse. The second mate and the wheelsman were there and, as it started to get very foggy, they started blowing the fog signals on the whistle. It wasn't long before the captain appeared and started walking back and forth in front of the wheelhouse. The second mate kept blowing the fog signal. A short time later the captain, walking back and forth in front of the open wheelhouse window said, "I say, I say, Buck, we are getting near Kagawong, I smell the cedars." After that, he walked to the ship's side, gave three pulls on the signal whistle to the engineroom. This was to check the engine down. He then came back to the open window and said, "Get the lines ready to tie up, Buck." He had his watch in his hand, at the open window he said to the wheelsman, "Hard-a-port." The wheelsman swung the wheel around a few turns, turning the ship to the left. The captain then said, "Steady." The wheelsman steadied the ship on a compass heading. The fog was still so thick I'm sure you could not see over fifty feet. In a matter of three or four minutes, we pulled alongside the dock at Kagawong. I told the foregoing story to make a comparison of the early days with the modern equipment they have for navigating today. Here was a captain with only a watch and magnetic compass and a lot of instinct. I have a great respect for a captain like this with his watch and magnetic compass and his great wealth of knowledge; he could smell his way through the fog.

HURONIC. 1929: H. Beaton, 1st Mate (centre), C. Stevens, Wheelsman (left), G. Lodge, Wheelsman (right)

3
CHAPTER

Captain at Last

In 1940, I was still first mate of the Noronic and this was to be the last season I would be first mate. We arrived in Port Arthur one Monday morning in July, and the district manager for Canada Steamship Lines met the Noronic on arrival. He told me to pack my bag and go over to Fort William and take the Huronic to Point Edward as captain. The master on the Huronic, Tom Johnston, was taken to hospital ill, and the Huronic was loaded with flour and feed for Point Edward. The Huronic no longer carried passengers and was on the package freight run, Sarnia to Lakehead. In those days, all ships had to be cleared in and out of port by Canada Customs. I got the necessary clearance and went to the Huronic at C.P.R. shed in Fort William. The first mate, Barney Wittaker and second mate, Waubie Pitfield on the Huronic, were very surprised to see me come aboard. I just said, "Get ready to sail, we are heading for Sarnia." Master at last and down the lakes we went.

I expected that one of the experienced captains would take over when we arrived at Point Edward and I would go back to my job as first

HURONIC — first ship launched from Collingwood Shipyards.
Sept. 12, 1901 (photo courtesy Collingwood Museum)

"Huronic", Port Arthur, Canada

Camera Shop Port Arthur
153

HURONIC at Port Arthur, Ont. (photo courtesy Lovelady
Camera Shop, Thunder Bay)

mate on the Noronic. No one came to relieve me at Point Edward and we loaded and headed west again. I still expected the company to send another captain to the Huronic. It was not the Canada Steamship Lines' policy to promote Northern Navigation mates to Captain of a Northern Navigation ship. They were always brought from the bulk boats and already had the experience being captain of the smaller boats. I continued as master of the Huronic into the fall season. It was a very stormy bad-weather fall. It being my first as captain, I had many decisions to make. Whether to go across Lake Superior on the regular course up the center or take the north shore or south shore, depending on the direction of the wind. We had plenty of rough water to contend with. The Huronic was a good ship in rough weather, well-built and lots of power. One trip downbound in November, 1940, we left Sault Ste. Marie with the wind so strong I had trouble getting turned to go down St. Mary's River. We had made the trip down the north shore of Lake Superior. After going down through to Canadian locks we had to turn and go to the new Ontario Dock at the Soo. We always fuelled up here as the Canada Steamship Lines had the Century Coal Dock here. It was in trying to turn to back down the river that I had a real struggle. The wind was so strong I could only get cross-way of the river. The Huronic, having real good power, we finally made the turn without running into the shore on the United States side. There are several narrow, buoyed channels in St. Mary's River and the wind was getting stronger every hour. I could not keep the ship from blowing sideways in these channels. we were going down the channel nearly crosswise and ducking around the marker buoys. I had the second mate take the steering from the wheelsman, who was doing very well, but I felt that the mate would know better what I was trying to do to keep the ship from blowing ashore out of the channel. We did make it to the lower St. Mary's River and found about seventy boats anchored in the shelter of the shore. I came off to the right at Lime Island and anchored in sheltered water under the land on the American side. The wind was so strong by now, I could not get the anchor to hold, so I dropped the second anchor. It was the first time in my life I had to use two anchors to try and hang on. It started to snow and became a blizzard. When I couldn't see a hundred feet in any direction, I didn't know if the anchors were holding or if we were drifting out of position. I had to keep the engine running and the wheelsman watched the compass and steered a course all night. Several times, we nearly blew around but, by steering and going half-speed on the engine, we were able to keep the ship heading into the shore. I couldn't see the shore and, knowing we were so close, I was afraid we would drag our anchors and run into the shore. The next day, the snow cleared and we found both anchors leading back on each side. They had a good hold of the bottom and hung on while we worked the engine to help hold us from blowing around. The wind was easing off and we were able to stop the engine, but we stayed anchored for another day before we left and went out on Lake Huron. Several ships on Lake Mighigan were in trouble during this storm. We heard distress calls over our radio telephone during the height of the storm.

I continued on the Huronic and finished the 1940 season and laid up in Sarnia. During the winter of 1941, I was working on inside repair and painting. About March 1, I received a contract from Canada Steamship Lines, Montreal, to be master of the Huronic. That pleased me very much as this was the first signed, sealed contract to be the captain of a ship. I must have satisfied the company that I was able to handle a ship. I heard several older captains were displeased at me getting the contract to sail the Huronic because I was younger and did not have the seniority. However, the company had a plan for us all. We fitted out at Sarnia and were on the package freight run to the Lakehead all that season. I hadn't run aground or knocked anything down and had a real good season, so I was again appointed to sail the Huronic in 1942.

We started our fit-out in Sarnia April 1, 1942. The Hamonic was to take the first trip April 6 out of Point Edward and the Huronic was to follow on the second trip a few days later. On April 6, things changed in a hurry for me. Capt. Atkin of the Noronic had just had an operation in Sarnia Hospital. He would not be able to sail the Noronic for the coming season. Capt. William Taylor already had the Hamonic loading at Point Edward shed. At noon on April 6, I was told to take over as master of Hamonic and Capt. Taylor was sent to the Noronic. That afternoon, I left Point Edward shed as captain of that beautiful ship I had admired so much. I could hardly believe that I was master of such a passenger-carrying ship at age thirty-nine. Believe me, I was real happy.

We made the run to Sault Ste. Marie uneventfully. But, as we passed up the Canadian lock at the Soo, I found that several big U.S. ships were stuck in the ice off Iroquois Point, starting into Whitefish Bay. They were all happy to see the Hamonic coming as she had good power and was a good ice breaker. The ice was very heavy — about three feet. I would run the Hamonic up alongside one of the three big bulk boats that was stuck. This would break up the ice around this ship and

HURONIC 1929

No 1093.
N.N. Cos. Str. Hamonic
Launched at Collingwood Nov. 6. 1908

HAMONIC *at Collingwood (photo courtesy Collingwood Museum)*

HAMONIC leaving Port Arthur, Ont. (photo courtesy Lovelady Camera Shop, Thunder Bay)

he was able to back up. The Hamonic would only go ahead about two boat lengths and I would back up and take another run at it. This went on all that day and we had only made a couple of miles ahead into this ice. We were now out in front of the fleet that had been stuck. In going ahead and backing up and taking another run at the ice, I was afraid I might do some damage to the ship. With full power and the ice so heavy the Hamonic could easily have broken her one inch steel bow plating. After it got dark, I quit ramming this ice and just stopped the engine and laid right in ice until daylight. We started the next morning and we could see dark patches in the ice, so we headed for these patches. The ice was a little softer in the dark patches and we were able to go ahead better. We got out to open water just inside Whitefish Point about four o'clock in the afternoon. By now, I was well ahead of the fleet that was stuck. We rounded Whitefish Point Light and put the ship on course for Passage island, 190 miles across Lake Superior. Open water all the way and we didn't run into any more ice until we rounded Thunder Cape and headed for the Welcome Islands and Port Arthur. We found that the tug Whalen, had cut a channel very nearly out to the Welcome Islands. We followed this channel into the breakwater. From the breakwater into the C.N.R. shed, Port Arthur, the ice was very heavy. By backing up and going ahead, we finally got tied up at C.N.R. shed, Port Arthur. This was the beginning of a good season on the Hamonic and everything turned out fine, as I had no trouble with the ship and maintained the schedule okay.

When you had a train schedule to meet, it kept you on the jump. The C.N.R. had a boat train from Port Arthur to Winnipeg at the west end and a boat train from Point Edward shed to Toronto Union Station. When the visibility was good, we had no trouble being on time; but, when it was thick fog, it was slow going. The boats didn't have radar at this time. We had a Gyro compass and direction finder and they were a help in the navigation, but it was slow tedious work. The 1924 season ended in mid-December and the Hamonic was laid up for the winter in Sarnia. I was appointed to go to the Hamonic again in 1943 and had another good season on the same run.

In 1944, I was again appointed to the Hamonic. This was a bad spring for ice again. Hamonic was a good ice-breaker breaking a channel in Whitefish Bay and helping the big bulk freight boats to open water. The following is an article written by Fred J. McGill, Duluth News Tribune Marine Editor: "A fleet of thirty-seven big bulk freighters of the Great Lakes broke out of ice and moved into open water at the east end of lake Superior last night and were putting on steam to get to Duluth, Superior Harbour for their initial cargoes of the 1944 season. This first ship is due at Duluth ship canal between three and six p.m. today. One by one late yesterday, the vessels veered into an almost clear path in twenty-one inch thick ice as the Canadian passenger steamer, Hamonic, a familiar visitor to Duluth, finally managed, after two days, to gain momentum enough to plow the ice apart. The Hamonic is sailing for Port Arthur, Ontario."

Hamonic was the first ship into Port Arthur in spring of 1944 and I won the traditional silk hat for opening the navigation season. This was the first time I had ever won the silk hat and I felt it was quite an honour. I am going to quote an article in the Port Arthur paper, Monday, April 10, 1944: "C.S.L. ship docks, early Sunday — Inching her way slowly through heavy ice in the harbour, the steamer, Hamonic, of the Northern Navigation Division of Canada Steamship Lines, moored at the C.N.R. dock at the foot of Arthur Street at 4:50 Sunday morning. The opening of navigation lacked much of the fanfare of other years. As the 5,265 ton ship came to rest at the dock, there were only two men, both policemen, to extend Capt. H.L. Beaton congratulations. But, for the captain, the fact that he had reached port first was a signal 'honour and achievement'. 'This is the first time in my twenty-four years on lake boats that I have been on a ship that opened navigation', the youthful, sandy-haired skipper said. This afternoon, he received the traditional silk 'topper' from officials of the Chamber of Commerce in recognition of his feat. Following closely on the 'heels' of the Hamonic was another Canada Steamship Lines ship, the Huronic, which docked here at 10:30, a stone's throw from her sister ship. Then, in fairly quick succession came several other ships, mostly grain carriers, which expect to load and return quickly from their first trip to the Lakehead. The ships were the Royalton, Colonial Steamship Company, which arrived at 11:30; Starbuck, Powell Steamship Company; Frontenac, Cleveland Cliffs Company; Capt. C.D. Secord, Mohawk Steamship Company, first in here on several other occasions; the George and Howard Hindeman, Hindeman Steamship Company; and the C.S.L. Prescott. The broad ice-covered bay echoed to the deep-throated sound of ships' whistles later in the morning as each new arrival was greeted by its predecessors, and busy tugs chugged back and forth, widening channels and preparing the way for a quick get-away for the ships leaving today or tomorrow. The harbour, deserted throughout the winter months, was crowded during afternoon and evening hours with men, women and children,

HAMONIC

bent on getting their first look at the Hamonic this year as she idled at the dock while stevedores emptied her ample hold. She carried a full cargo of general merchandise. 'The trip was fairly plain sailing once we cleared the ice in Whitefish Bay', Capt. Beaton recounted. 'We passed Whitefish Point at noon Saturday and the Welcome Islands at 3:05 this morning. The ship struck hard ice twenty-five minutes later, but by jogging around a bit and sticking to the channel cut by tugs, we managed to negotiate the rest of the journey without much difficulty. Biggest trouble was outside of the C.N.R. dock where heavy ice made mooring difficult. The trip from Whitefish Point to the dock took slightly less than seventeen hours. The Hamonic left Sarnia at 6:00 p.m. last Tuesday, had an uneventful passage across Lake Huron, but ran into heavy ice in the lower St. Mary's River, where several boats were stuck and some had damaged propellers. We went around one damaged boat, which was holding up the others and worked our way to the Soo. When the ship reached the upper St. Mary's ice as thick as twenty-one inches was encountered. The Hamonic continued bucking ice, together with

the William H. Donner and the Colonel J. Picklands, both ore carriers on the way to Duluth-Superior for their first cargo of 1944 season. We made about five miles in four days. Then, the car ferry, Saint Marie, a good ice breaker, was sent from the Straits of mackinaw to help open up a channel through Whitefish Bay.'

Capt. Beaton took over command of his ship three years ago. The silk topper he received this afternoon will be exchanged for an order at any store here for the purchase of any hat in the establishment. The Chief Engineer, James Neilon, was presented with a box of cigars.'

The car ferry cut a channel to open water and the Hamonic was able to follow this channel better than the big ore carriers. They were longer and, if the channel cut by the car ferry turned sharply, the big ships would get stuck on the turn. The Hamonic was able to reach open water quite a long way ahead of the rest of the fleet.

We loaded flour and feed for Point Edward and departed. The rest of 1944 season was the same routine run and was made uneventful and the Hamonic was again laid up for winter months in Sarnia.

Tug frees lake freighters trapped in Georgian Bay ice (photo courtesy Star Weekly, Toronto April 21, 1951)

4
CHAPTER

"Fire"

HAMONIC on fire, July 17, 1945. Point Edward, Ont.

I was appointed to the Hamonic again in 1945. This season, the run was the same and we were well into the summer schedule when tragedy caught up to the Hamonic that would end the career of a beautiful passenger ship. We had completed our eastbound trip and were in Windsor, Ontario, on Friday July 16. We loaded freight and passengers and left Windsor at 9:00 p.m., went across the river to Detroit to take on more passengers for our westbound trip. We departed Detroit at 11:00 p.m. for our trip up Detroit River, across Lake St. Clair and up the St. Clair River to our dock at Point Edward. We tied up at 5:00 a.m. and always tried to make the least noise or fuss, trying not to disturb the 230 passengers we had taken aboard the night before. I had always navigated the Hamonic from Detroit to Point Edward myself, letting the mates have a rest. As soon as we had the ship tied up at Point Edward, I went to bed in my room just below the wheelhouse on top deck. The loading started at 7:00 a.m. Saturday morning July 17, 1945; the gangplanks from ship to dock were put in. Four gangways were used and the shed doors were opened on the dockside, as well as all the shed doors open on the track side. This gave access to all the box car loads of freight put alongside the shed by C.N.R. The freight shed was about 1000 feet long and of wood construction. The Hamonic was tied up at the north half of this shed, since this was where the westbound package freight was loaded. The south half of the shed contained flour and feed cargoes eastbound. The package freight was loaded out of box cars and piled on pallet boards. These pallet boards are handled by fork-lift trucks and loaded aboard ship. One of these fork-lift trucks operated by a gasoline engine was not working well. The operator took it back to the repair room about the center of the shed on the side next to the dock. In trying to improve the operation of this truck, the operator advanced the spark on the distributor, which caused the engine to backfire through the carburetor. This set the gas in the carburetor on fire. The operator ran out into the shed looking for a fire extinguisher. We had fire extinguishers at every gangway on the ship. The first mate, "Waubie" Pitfield, got one fire extinguisher out and went to the next gangway and took another extinguisher out into the shed. The fire in the carburetor of the machine was burning right under the gasoline tank on the lift-truck. Suddenly, the gas tank exploded and flaming gasoline was blown all over the shed. The fire spread very quickly. So quickly, the workers said, they couldn't run fast enough to keep ahead of it as they ran out of the shed. When Pitfield saw the extent of the fire, he just dropped the second fire extinguisher and then ran up the stairs on four decks to get to my room, waking me up and yelling, "The shed is on

fire!" I jumped into my pants over the pyjamas and headed through the lower wheelhouse and up the ladder to the wing of the bridge and upper wheelhouse. I could see that all the lifeboats on the dock side were on fire, as well as the afterhouse behind the smoke stack. I turned on the alarm, also blew the emergency signal on the ship's whistle. I rang the engine room telegraph, double full astern. By now, there was a complete cover of black smoke. I couldn't see anything of the burning shed or any part of the ship aft of the wheelhouse. The engineer answered my signal and gave the engine full astern. Mooring lines, gangplanks were all torn loose from the dock. I backed the ship out into the river, knowing that when the stern would get into the downbound current, she would back down the river. Once out into the river, we were then clear of the blanket of black smoke. All the top deck behind the wheelhouse was on fire and I could see wheelsman, John Kent, trying to get out the fire hose at his station ahead of the first lifeboat. The lifeboat covers were all on fire and the wood-covered canvas dome on top deck, aft of the observation room, was also on fire. John Kent did not stay there very long. As the Hamonic was backing down the river, I saw a Steel Trust ship upbound not far away. This ship started blowing danger signals. I didn't pay too much attention to the danger signals, as I was in more trouble than he was.

I didn't know just what to do. With the extent of the fire on the ship and knowing that the ship had passengers and crew on board, I had to get the ship close to shore so they would have a chance to get off. I rang the engine-room telegraph to full ahead and took hold of the wheel. Luckily, the steam steering gear was on and I could steer the ship. Just off to my right on the shore was Purdy's Fish Dock and above that, the Century Coal Dock where there was a slight indentation on the shore, a former ferry dock. I steered the Hamonic full speed, bow first, into this coal dock and that put the Purdy Fish Dock not far off the starboard (right) side.

She was stuck in there fairly solid. By now, the after house and deck behind the wheelhouse was on fire and everything was getting very hot. I went out of the wheelhouse, down the ladder to the next deck. Everything was on fire on this deck. The cabin walls were steel construction and had several coats of white paint. I couldn't believe that could burn like it did. I could see the whole white painted wall crinkle and curl with the heat and then burst into flame. I jumped over the rail and into the river about twenty feet below. After I came to the surface, I started swimming to the coal dock. Once on the dock at the front end of

HAMONIC on fire, July 17, 1945. Point Edward, Ont.

the ship, I could see some heads right in the very nose of the ship. The whirley with steel bucket for loading coal was able to turn and the operator put his boom up to the front of the ship. He could drop his clam bucket on the deck and he had taken off several people; they got into the bucket and he hoisted it, swung it and lowered it onto the deck. This boom was up to the front of the ship when I got on the dock. I went over to it and climbed up to the deck. There were two older women there and I helped them into the bucket. They were landed on the dock this way. I came back down the boom again to the dock. I was standing looking up at the burning ship and a lady came up to me and said, "Can I treat those burns?" I didn't know I had any burns, but the back of my hand, the end of my nose, my right hand, high cheek and the edge of my right ear were burned.

Reflecting on the fire later, I discovered that I could not have put the Hamonic in a much better spot. Alongside Purdy's Dock, there were two steel scows, used for setting pond nets. They were able to loosen these scows and shove them out alongside the ship where the gangway doors to the freight deck were open. With the noise of putting in gangplanks to start loading package freight at the shed, most of the passengers were up and in the dining room for breakfast. In talking to a man and woman who were passengers, after they had been taken ashore in one of the scows, they recalled that they were at a table in the dining room on the dock side. The lady was sitting next to the dining room window and the side of the shed would be only twenty-five feet away from her across the dock. Her husband was sitting next to her at the table. She said to him, "Look, that shed is on fire." Then, all the plate glass windows in the dining room on the dock side just exploded. This would happen when the intense heat hit them. They all went out the main dining room doors and down the main stairs. This led right down to the freight deck where the gangway doors were open. Purdy and his men were able to shove the steel scows alongside these open doors so all they had to do was step onto the scow and the scow was pushed ashore. The freight deck overhead is all steel, built that way to carry the decks above. The fire was in the decks and cabins above the freight deck, leaving this area free from fire or smoke. The passengers were in the best place they could be. They had time to take off several loads until all were off the ship.

Other passengers and crew had gone to both ends of the ship, as the fire had not worked its way to either end. They had rope lines to slide down into the water. Some jumped off and were picked up by a couple of small boats that had come alongside. The most of those who were hurt had burned hands, as sliding down a rope, the rope goes through your hands fast and can cause severe burns. I was talking to Dr. W.B. Carruthers, who was and had been the company doctor for several years. He told me that there is always a funny side to something tragic. We had a crew of girls, mostly university girls on their summer holidays, working as waitresses in the dining room. These girls had light salmon-coloured uniforms. In the middle of July, they didn't have much on under this uniform. The doctor laughingly told me they were giving these girls first aid for rope burns, as they all grabbed a rope, wrapped their legs around the rope and slid down. "Well," the doctor said, "they are all embarassed when we have to treat the burns between their legs!"

There was a big crowd of people on the dock by now and I started looking around for the Chief Engineer, Jim Neilon. I couldn't see him, so I had one of Purdy's fish boats take me to the outboard engine room gangway door, which was open. I could see the chief and two or three of his men were still inside the engine room. We got them out on the small boat and the chief looked up to see the whole top of the ship was on fire. He said, "I nearly fainted, I had no idea the fire was so bad." That ended the sailing career of the Hamonic, the most beautiful passenger ship on the lakes. I admired this ship above all the rest. She was eventually towed to Windsor and cut up for scrap.

HAMONIC (photo courtesy of Paisley Collection, Sarnia)

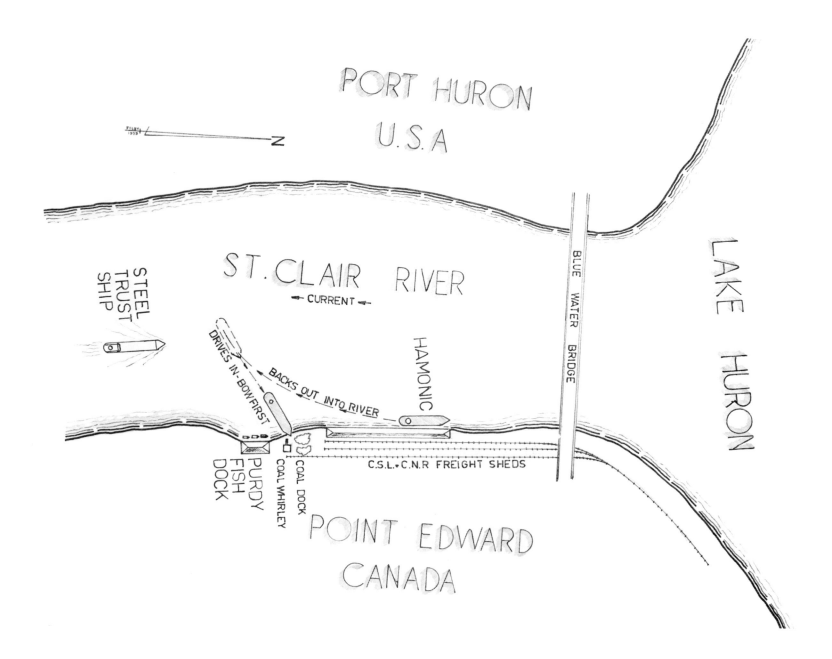

PORT HURON
U.S.A

FILOVI
1978
N

ST. CLAIR RIVER
← CURRENT →

STEEL
TRUST
SHIP

LAKE HURON

BLUE WATER BRIDGE

DRIVES IN-BOW FIRST
BACKS OUT INTO RIVER

HAMONIC

PURDY FISH DOCK
COAL WHIRLEY
COAL DOCK

C.S.L.•C.N.R FREIGHT SHEDS

POINT EDWARD
CANADA

49

THIS DRAMATIC PHOTOGRAPH shows how most of the 247 passengers of the Hamonic made their escape as fire swept the ship. The ship was cut adrift and a coal crane was brought into use to lift the passengers, five at a time, to the top of a 35-foot coal pile. Two women getting ready to come down landing ropes are seen at the bow of the ship

Crane Operator Who Saved Many From Hamonic

One of the many heroes of the fire which destroyed the lake cruise ship Hamonic at Point Edward yesterday was Mr. Elmer Kleinsmith, crane operator of the Century Coal Company. Aided by Mr. Bill Meeson, Canada Steamship Lines employe, Mr. Kleinsmith moved his huge crane close enough to the burning vessel for the bucket to be swung to the bow. Frantic passengers crowded into the shovel, then the crane operator would lower it to shore. In this manner more than 50 persons were taken off the Hamonic at the height of the fire. Above, the crane operator is seen standing beside the coal bucket which provided an aerial path to safety for so many passengers. *(Star Staff Photo.)*

The last person to leave the Hamonic as she burned at the docks at Point Edward yesterday morning was the chief engineer, Mr. James Neilson, above. Mr. Neilson stayed on board to direct engine room work until the ship had grounded.

Hamonic Captain Congratulated On Handling Of Ship During Fire

SARNIA, July 17 — "Captain Horace Beaton is to be congratulated on his fine presence of mind in handling the Hamonic when it burst into flames this morning," said Leroy Owen, of Minneapolis, Minn., who was a passenger aboard the ship when the accident occurred.

"The captain had the cables tying the ship to the dock loosed. Then he backed the Hamonic away from the flames on shore and rammed her hard into the land away from the fire, grounding her so that people ashore could aid those in danger to get off the boat.

Mr. Owen himself stayed on the ship until he had assisted more than 20 excited passengers down a rope at the bow. He told reporters how he had helped at least three persons with infants in their arms slide down the ropes. With one arm they held their child and used the other to ease themselves and their youngster to safety.

Capt. Beaton Saved Many, Hamonic Crewman Says

Capt. Horace Beaton of the Steamer Hamonic was definitely responsible for saving the lives of many passengers on board during the fire last Tuesday morning, Don Leaney, 16, son of Squadron Leader C. P. Leaney, representative of the War Assets Corporation here, and a bus boy on the steamer, declared in an interview Saturday.

The youth who was making his first trip, said Capt. Beaton was badly burned on the bridge while he was beaching the vessel. The wheelhouse was burning under him, blocking his escape, so he dove 60 feet into the water.

Capt. Beaton, stated young Leaney, crawled up the arm of a coal shovel used to unload vessels and got back into the ship where he personally assisted many in getting off. He was the last to leave the burning hulk. All this time the captain was clad only in his pyjamas.

Relating his own experience during the fire, Don said he was in the dining room and walked back to the kitchen with a tray of breakfast dishes. When he returned the whole side of the boat was crackling with flames and smoke was infiltrating into the room.

Humor was injected into the scene in the face of tragedy. He told of a waitress trying to calm the passengers, and then going to the kitchen to shout, "a single fried." Meanwhile flames licked into the dining room.

The passengers were cleared out of the dining room on the promenade deck and most of them ran wherever they wanted, said the youth. The majority went below to the next deck.

"A few passengers became panicky and went below locking themselves in their state rooms," he said. "The crew had to break down the doors to get them out."

Don ran around to the freight deck and slid down a rope into the water where he was picked up almost immediately by a U.S. coast guard cutter.

After the fire

5
CHAPTER

After the Fire

Two weeks after the fire, the operating manager wrote me a letter telling me to go on the Huronic. Tom MacLeod was the captain of the Huronic and was not in the best of health. They put me on the "Huronic to help him, if and when he didn't feel well. I went aboard around August 1 and put in the rest of 1945 season running up and down the lakes. That was the best job I ever had, as I had hardly anything to do. The Huronic laid up in December, 1945, in Sarnia.

The following spring, 1946, I was wondering what job or ship I would get. I finally got a contract agreement to be captain of the S.S. Lethbridge, a canal-size package freighter running from Montreal to lakehead. Then, I received a letter from the C.S.L. operating manager, telling me that Capt. MacLeod was in hospital in Owen Sound. They had sent him a contract to be captain of the Huronic again. MacLeod was too ill and wouldn't be able to go back to work. So, I would be going on the Huronic for the 1946 season. Capt. MacLeod didn't come back to the Huronic and never sailed again.

In the spring of 1947, I was back on the Huronic on the same run. We were downbound in July and I turned below Soo Locks and went to our coal dock to take on fuel. The agent for Canada Steamship Lines at Soo came to the ship and told me I would have to get off and return to Port Arthur by train. The first mate, Roy Maher, was to take the Huronic on to Sarnia. Capt. Taylor of the Noronic was ill and in hospital at Port Arthur. I was to go Captain on the Noronic when she returned from Duluth on her scheduled trip east. They had a bulk boat captain take the Noronic over to Duluth. The Noronic arrived back in Port Arthur on Saturday morning and was to leave on schedule at 1:00 p.m. for Sault Ste. Marie, Sarnia, Detroit and Windsor. I got aboard and we left on time. This was back to the passenger run again, but I was familiar with the Noronic and had no trouble handling the big ship. That was the latter part of July, 1947, right in the middle of the summer passenger schedule for the Noronic. We still had August and to the middle of September to put in on the summer schedule. I expected Capt. Taylor to be back to take over again, but his illness kept him from coming back to his ship and I carried on.

The Noronic had several post season cruises to make. We were to take a cruise out of Detroit to Mackinac Island and Sault Ste. Marie and

NORONIC after wheelhouse was closed in.

S.S. COLLINGWOOD leaving Soo Lock upbound, 1950

FORT HENRY — the first of the 'fort' ships

return. When I got to Mackinac Island, the weather was bad, blowing gale force winds. The storm warnings were flying and I checked down outside Mackinac Island. I had a decision to make. With the high superstructure on the Noronic and the wind blowing forty-five to fifty miles per hour off the dock (*Great Lakes sailors used miles per, rather than knots*), I could picture the trouble I could get into. Another boat was already at the dock, and the "Norry" was uncontrollable at low speed and tight quarters. I didn't like to see the passengers miss this beautiful island resort but, if I missed making the dock and the ship blew aground, it would end the trip for them right there. I decided not to try it. I would go on to Sault Ste. Marie and go up through the locks and make a trip up to Whitefish Bay. This was not on the schedule, but would fill in some time and some scenery for the passengers. We turned around off Iroquois Point and came back down through the Canadian lock at the Soo. We tied up at the New Ontario dock at the Soo for the rest of that night. We left the next day on our scheduled time on the return trip to Detroit. In addition, the Noronic had a post season cruise to Midland, Ontario, in the Georgian Bay. This gave the passengers a chance to visit Martyr's Shrine and Huron Village, historic landmarks of that area. I thought that the Noronic would tie up for the season when we finished these trips, but the company decided to keep her in the package freight run from Point Edward to Lakehead. The Noronic was a real good ship in the fall weather. I had a few struggles to make the dock at times when the wind was strong. The high superstructure of the Noronic would catch a lot of wind and blow sideways as soon as you slowed down. We sailed right up to the end of the season on 1947 and tied up for the winter in Sarnia about the middle of December.

Capt. Taylor returned to the Noronic and for the seasons of 1948 and 1949, I was on the same run with the Huronic. We were westbound, going across lake Huron on the morning of September 17, 1949, when I got down to the dining room; the crew already there asked me if I heard the news about the Noronic? They said she was on fire and burning at her dock in Toronto. I soon went back to my room and radio. The news was bad, a lot of lives lost. I was sick at my stomach because I had been through the fire on the Hamonic. We were very lucky not to have had any loss of life. That ended the sailing career of another fine passenger ship.

The season of 1949 came to an end with the last trip from Lakehead to Point Edward with flour and feed cargo. They told me then that, as soon as we were unloaded, I was to take the Huronic to Hamilton. I took the Huronic down the Welland Canal for the first and last time in her career. We tied up at C.S.L. freight shed, Hamilton, and I knew that she was very close to the Steel Company dock, where they cut up the ships for scrap. The Huronic was getting too expensive to run. She was nearly fifty years old and with four hand-fired boilers, she was just costing too much to operate. Also, she had a wooden cabin and superstructure, so everything added up. That was the end of the three passenger ships of the Northern Navigation Division of Canada Steamship Lines. It was a sorry thought to me that I was the last captain of two of them. The Huronic was scrapped early in 1950 and the S.S. Manitoba of Canadian Pacific passenger fleet was also scrapped in Hamilton about the same time.

All during the winter of 1949-1950, I was wondering what was in store for me. They would have to have some different package freight boats on the Northern Navigation run. The Canada Steamship Lines took two of the smaller bulk freight boats, the Collingwood and Martian, and made them into package freight carriers. This change-over was done at the Midland ship yards, which were owned by Canada Steamship Lines. They built a "tween" deck, that is, another deck below the main deck, and cut side doors on both sides of the ships. This allowed loading through the side doors also, and an elevator from the top deck to lower cargo hold. Also, the bulkheads between cargo holds were cut to allow lift trucks with pallet boards loaded with cargo to pass back and forth in loading and unloading.

I was appointed to the Collingwood in the opening of 1950 season. We were to run on the same run — Windsor, Sarnia to Lakehead — with package freight and we had flour and feed as well as newsprint paper to carry eastbound. We carried paper into Cleveland and Toledo in ohio, also into Detroit for both Detroit Free Press and Detroit News. The paper was loaded at Great Lakes Paper Mill in Fort William. The paper mill was as far up the Kaministiqua River as the ship could go and many a load we took out of this dock in Fort William. Also, we would load at the Abitibi Paper Mill, located east of Port Arthur Harbour on Thunder Bay. I always liked the paper cargoes — they were clean and always smelled fresh from the wood the paper was made from. We had another paper mill to load at, the Domtar Mill at Red Lock. We would run up to the north shore of Lake Superior and go in to Nipigon Bay and through the islands to Red Rock dock, not far from the town of Nipigon, Ontario. At this dock, we loaded boxboard paper. This is a heavy brown paper used in making cardboard cartons.

Industry uses cardboard cartons to package most of its manufactured goods. The trip in and out of Red Rock was always interesting, as the islands were all high land and very scenic. When we had this trip to make in dense fog, it wasn't so interesting. We had radar by now and believe me, it was a real help to us in navigating these narrow waters.

I was appointed to Collingwood for the seasons of 1951 through 1954. We had the same package freight run and the two bulk boats that the company remodelled to carry package freight were working out very well. The package freight trade was flourishing and Canada Steamship Lines decided to build new package freight boats. The lower St. Lawrence Seaway was being built and that would allow larger ships to trade to Montreal. The first new package freight boat was built in Collingwood and they planned to build six more. Five of these ships would be named after old forts in Canada. The S.S. Fort Henry was completed and ready to sail in the spring of 1955. She was a lovely streamlined ship, 460 feet long with a steam turbine engine and automatic oil-fired boilers. She was fast too, could do eighteen miles an hour plus. Compared to the old package freight boats, which would run at about twelve miles per hour and had hand-fired coal-burning boilers, the new "Fort Henry" was a beauty.

Capt. Roy Anderson was appointed master of the Fort Henry and that left the Martian open. So, I asked to be transferred to the Martian, where the Chief Engineer was Jimmy Neilon, my old friend from the Hamonic. Jimmy was one of those outdoor guys who liked fishing. Many a good day we had together on a trout stream in the Lakehead area. On one of our fishing trips to one of the small streams north west of Port Arthur, we were walking single file along the bank of the stream. We were going through tag alder or brush about five feet high on this trail. Jimmy was ahead of me and had his fishing rod under his arm and was tying on a new hook. All of a sudden, he fell back and nearly knocked me down. I didn't know what hit him, but right in front of him was a black and white animal with a white fog rising from it. I soon knew the reason for Jimmy's fast move astern. Luckily for him, his fast move saved him from getting sprayed. We made a detour around this obstacle and went on fishing.

I continued on the Martian for 1956 and 1957. On one trip in November of 1956, we were upbound on Lake Huron with seventeen automobiles on the top deck. The cars were driven on board and lined up in rows. None of them were fastened down, only the brake set on solid. We had passed Harbour Beach Light when we started getting a strong northeast wind and it began building up a big sea, about fifteen foot waves. This required me to change the course heading into this sea to keep the ship from rolling too heavily. We had passed abeam of point Aux Barques Light and we were in a position that Lake Huron could get a long swat at us from the northeast. We kept ploughing along all night making only about two miles per hour ahead. The wind started to veer back to the northwest and we were getting a big sea from the two directions. I had a hard job trying to keep the ship from turning around into the trough of the sea. I knew if the ship got into the trough, it would roll so hard that those seventeen automobiles would go over the side. We hung on and were able to keep the ship headed into the sea.

At eight o'clock in the morning, we were still getting a sea coming at us from both the port and starboard sides. The third mate and wheelsman came to relieve the first mate and wheelsman on watch. They had been able to get back the deck to the galley and forward again. The cook was having his troubles getting breakfast ready. They had to hold the coffee pot onto the stove and only had a hand-out to eat. I saw the first mate, Art Ostrander, get back the deck by bracing himself and hanging on to everything he could get hold of. I decided I would forego breakfast; no way was I going to try and make it back to galley and back up forward again. I happened to be looking out the back windows of the wheelhouse when I saw the first mate come out the galley door and start up the deck with his coat buttoned up and his head down. At the same time, a big wave came over the port side and started back the deck. It was quite a body of water heading for the first mate coming up the deck. Art suddenly saw that wave of water coming toward him. He was right opposite a steel door leading to the upper boiler room, but this door was closed and I saw him trying to open this door without success. The wave was getting closer to him and, in desperation, he turned and reached up over his head and grabbed the rungs of a ladder that was made fast and led down from top deck to spar deck. The first mate, being short and stout and reaching up for the ladder, pulled in his big stomach just as the wave of water hit him. The wave passed him and went along the afterhouse and steel bulwarks, right aft and over the stern. It took one of his shoes right overboard at the stern and took his pants right down around his ankles. Even though there was an element of danger in the situation, I had to laugh at the sight of him, hanging on to the ladder rung for dear life. He finally composed himself, got his pants back up and made it up the deck okay. We finished the season of 1956 and I continued as captain of the Martian for the season of 1957 in the same package freight run.

MARTIAN (photo courtesy, McNutt Photo, Detroit)

FORT YORK launching, January 15, 1958 (photo courtesy Schuller Fotography)

6
CHAPTER

The Fort York

There was another new "Fort" package freighter being built in Collingwood. The S.S. Fort York was a different design. The wheelhouse was built back aft forward of the smoke stack. She was 461 feet long and had four side doors on each side. For loading package freight, there were elevators from the "tween" deck to each cargo hold. On top deck, the hatches were large and counter sunk into the deck to allow automobiles, trucks and buses to run up and down a flat surface. This ship had automatic oil-fired boilers and a steam-driven turbine engine.

I was given command of this new ship. We went out of Collingwood early in April, 1958, on the trial run. The shipyard had their own captain take her out, so I had nothing to do but watch. We ran over near Griffith Island, where a measured mile had been set out on the shore. They ran past these markers using a stop watch to take the time at full speed, up toward Cape Croker and back again past the markers. She was real fast and did around nineteen miles per hour on these trial trips. We had about sixty extra passengers aboard — shipyard officials, company officials, shipyard engineers, technicians and some invited guests. The company wanted to get this ship in operation as soon as possible, so they decided not to return to Collingwood with all these extra passengers aboard. They arranged to have the Canadian Government boat that was putting all aids to navigation into operation come alongside and take all the extra passengers off and return them to Collingwood. That left our own crew aboard and they said to me, "She is all yours, take her away." Now, I was the Captain and I gave the engineroom "full ahead" and headed her off on a course that would take us out of Georgian Bay and down Lake Huron to Sarnia. On a course out of Georgian Bay, we passed very close to Flower Pot Island and we made a sharp turn to the left. When I put the steering wheel over to make this turn, the ship was running full out and heeled over. I thought I had a tiger by the tail! I had never been on anything so fast. We made the Point Edward shed and I was quite proud of my new ship. Being right close to home, the family were all on hand to greet me and take a look around the new ship. We proceeded down the Welland Canal to Toronto. We tied up at C.S.L. Dock, Pier #9 at the foot of Yonge Street. The company had their new package freighter on display and held open house for a day to all those who shipped freight and their friends.

FORT YORK maiden trip. Toronto 1958. C.S.L. (Vice Pres.) Cresswell and Capt. Horace Beaton

Deck of the FORT YORK tied up in Welland Canal (photo courtesy Carl Turnquist. Detroit)

We continued to run package freight westbound and we carried grain east to Kingston elevator. The lower St. Lawrence Seaway was not open yet, but expected to open for the season of 1959. This run continued through the summer months of 1958 and we were unloading grain at Kingston elevator on September 10. That morning, I felt ill. We expected to be finished unloading at noon. We left Kingston elevator about two o'clock in the afternoon. I was able to take the ship out of Kingston. The weather was beautiful — clear and calm — and I was glad to turn the ship over to the second mate and he could head her up Lake Ontario to Hamilton. I went to bed. By now, everything was turning upside down. I was quite dizzy and was glad to lie down. About 5:00 p.m., I called the first mate, Carl Norton, down to my room; he was on watch at four o'clock. I told him he would have to send a message to C.S.L. agent in Hamilton and give him our E.T.A. as midnight, and ask him to have the company doctor meet the ship on arrival. Carl would have to take the ship into the C.S.L. shed in Hamilton. He said, "I have never handled a ship into dock before." When he got into Hamilton Harbour and heading for the shed, he found a suction dredge working with the pipeline from the dredge right across the entrance to the shed. He had to stop and try and hold the ship in position while they got the tender boat to break the pipeline so the ship could proceed into the shed dock. He did a real good job docking the ship.

Doctor Hutchison was there to meet the ship and he looked me over and said he was sending for an ambulance to take me to Hamilton General Hospital. I was admitted around 1:00 a.m. and the doctor started blood transfusions. I was hemorrhaging internally and had lost a lot of blood. I didn't have a pain or an ache, but was very weak. They gave me two pints of blood and the next night, I had a hemorrhage by mouth. I guess I nearly passed on as I was out like a light. The doctor told me the next afternoon that he didn't know if he was going to save my life. I reacted favourably to the coagulation needles they were giving me and the hemorrhage was stopped. The doctor said if I had been a heavy drinker, the blood would be thin and would not coagulate and I would have bled to death. They kept the blood transfusions going and I shall be forever indebted to the Red Cross, as they provided the necessary blood to keep me alive. They gave me twelve pints all told. After about ten days, they x-rayed me and found I had an ulcer in the side wall of the stomach and it had penetrated through the wall of the stomach and into an artery. They operated on me around September 23 and took out about one third of my stomach. They did a good job on me as twenty years later, I have had no trouble in that respect. I was able to leave the hospital about the middle of October and did not go back on the boat to finish that season. That gave me all winter to recuperate and I was able to go back to the Fort York in the spring of 1959.

This season, the lower St. Lawrence Seaway was opened and we extended our run to Montreal and back west again to the lakehead. The new Seaway let the big bulk boats down to Montreal and they could carry their cargoes of grain to Montreal and farther east down the Gulf. This spelled the end of the canal boats. They were of a size capable of getting through the small locks, and it would take ten canal boats carrying 100,000 bushels of grain each to one cargo of the 730 foot boats of today. They will carry over 1,000,000 bushels in one load. Labrador iron ore is transported back up through the Seaway and this makes a good trade for the big boats. The smaller canal boats have very nearly all disappeared and a new era of big ships has taken over, both inland and salt water.

One memory of the Fort York was on a trip up the Welland Canal. Our radio telephone was always open on a channel that you could hear all the conversations between the ships. This particular night, we were upbound in the Welland Canal and the canal is not very wide. Two ships meeting have to be very careful not to come together or to get too close to the canal bank when passing. One of the canal-size tankers was downbound meeting an upper laker, upbound. Maybe the canal boat didn't get over as far as he could have and the upper laker felt that he had crowded him. Over the radio telephone, we heard the upper laker call the tanker and give him a tongue lashing for not giving him enough room in passing. There was a French captain on the tanker and he came on the air and said, "What the hell you want me to do, take the highway?" There was a road alongside the canal, so we all had a laugh.

No wonder the small canal boat has gone. The 730 foot ships of today carry so much more cargo and have more power, are faster and everything is more automated. They are able to carry less crew. I read some statistics a few years ago that it takes 51,000 acres of prairie land to grow one load for the big ships of today. Also, it takes 865 box cars by railroad to transport that same amount of grain from the west to the Lakehead. Today, the big salt water ships come all the way inland to the Lakehead to load this grain and take it to any port in the world. The new St. Lawrence Seaway made this possible. The big lake boats take these cargoes to Montreal and Quebec and Port Cartier on the Gulf of St. Lawrence. It is transshipped into salt water boats for all over the world. The Labrador iron ore coming inland makes a cargo for the lake boats westbound. Being in a ship that carried package freight, I never had the opportunity to have any of these big grain or iron ore cargoes. The Fort York was on the run from Montreal west with package freight. Eastbound, we carried newsprint paper, box board paper, flour and feed and all kinds of package freight. I continued on this ship for 1960 on the same run.

FORT YORK at Hamilton, Ontario

FORT CHAMBLY, launched in snow storm (photo courtesy Schuller Fotography)

7
CHAPTER

The Fort Chambly

During the winter of 1960-61, I was notified that I was to be captain on a new ship being built in Collingwood. This ship was the M.V. Fort Chambly. The christening of this ship was in March, 1961, and my wife and I were invited to attend. It was a cold day and the christening was at the ship lying in the dry dock. I know we didn't linger too long in the cold. The ship had been launched the previous December and was now nearly completed. They had a social hour inside the shipyard building and this was followed by a luncheon at a church hall. They had several speakers and the president of the Steel Company of Canada was thanking Collingwood Shipbuilding Company for the wonderful new ship they had built for the Steel Company. My wife, listening to this speech, turned to me and said, "I thought you worked for the Canada Steamship Lines. How come you are to be the captain on this ship belonging to the Steel Company of Canada?" I was at a loss to get the connection, too. The Steel Company built the ship and had the Canada Steamship Lines operate the ship for them. In three years time, the Canada Steamship Lines took over the ship and the registry was changed to Canada Steamship Lines, as owners.

This ship was similar in design to the Fort York. The wheelhouse and accomodation were aft and the deck was flush, no raised hatches. She had a deck crane to lift the steel hatches. The flush deck was good for carrying cars, trucks and buses. There were four gangway doors on each side for loading package freight and there were hydraulic elevators into each cargo hold from the "tween" deck. We went on the trial trip on April 5, 1961, and ran the measured mile north of Griffith Island. This ship was all automated with pilot-house control of the engines. This was something new for me, as I was always used to having the engineer operate the engine, ahead or astern. The Chambly had four diesel engines on a reduction gear to one shaft and propellor. The propeller hadfour variable pitch blades and these blades were hydraulically controlled. The blades would turn from the ahead pitch to the astern pitch and the amount of pitch you put on the blade gave you the speed you required. I understand that the Chambly was the first ship on the Great Lakes to have the variable pitch propellor. the engines can be controlled from any of three positions in the spacious wheelhouse. This ship was handled with ease. It put me in mind of driving an old gear

FORT CHAMBLY Christening, March 1961

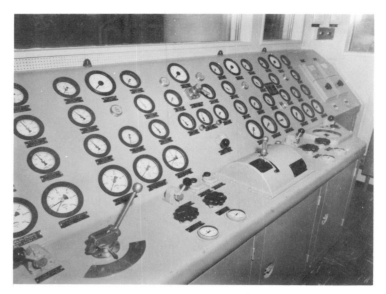

FORT CHAMBLY engine room control panel

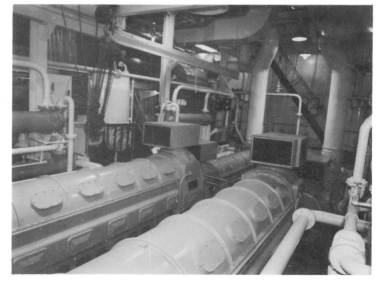

FORT CHAMBLY engine room

FORT CHAMBLY in Welland Canal

FORT CHAMBLY Wheelhouse control

FORT CHAMBLY Wheelhouse chart table

shift car then driving a new automatic. The master in the wheelhouse can do everything except lower the anchor and put out the mooring lines to tie up to the dock. Electronic sounding, radar, direction finder, gyro compass and automatic steering make navigating the ship easier. You can get the required power from the engines with the movement of a small lever and one hand. The handling of the engines can be turned over to the engineer in case any of the automated equipment gets fouled up. The captain then signals the engineer what he requires to manoeuvre the ship. When the ship is set on a straight course, you can turn over the manual steering to automatic. The automatic pilot, worked in connection with the gyro compass, can steer better than a man. There is no human error of using too much wheel, as the automatic pilot gives just the required rudder to keep the ship on a straight course.

Occasionally, these automatic controls fail and in the first month after starting out on the Fort Chambly, I had a bad time with these automatic controls for the engines. On her maiden trip, we were approaching the Welland Canal downbound. I checked the speed after passing the big sea buoy off Port Colborne. We went through the breakwater entrance to Welland Canal, still running on one engine. I was a couple of boat lengths inside when I began to slow the one engine down. Ahead, were two bridges, number twenty-one and twenty across the canal at Port Colborne. I eased the control lever back and found the revolutions remained the same and the pitch on the propeller blades

FORT CHAMBLY Wheelhouse

didn't change. This kept the ship running at a good clip. I changed to astern to back up and slow down. Number two engine cuts in automatically, so you have two engines always on the back up. This is a safety measure to assure you won't stall the number one engine and have nothing. When I put the lever in the astern position and got the power of two engines, we shot ahead when we should have been backing up. I put the lever back to stop and had the same number one engine going ahead, still very fast. I was getting closer to the two bridges and they were still closed across the canal. I sent the third mate up to the bow deck to drop both anchors. It was rocky in that part of the canal and I could hear the anchors rattling over the bottom, no use at all to stop the ship. If I had thrown my hat overboard, it would have had the same effect. I gave the signal to the engine room for full astern. The engineer was always standing by to take over the control of the engines if I ever used this signal. He took over the control and made the required moves to put the engines full astern. But we got all four engines full ahead and we were getting very close to the bridges. I was just going to direct the wheelsman to steer the ship into the cement piers of the old canal. We would smash up our own bow, but save the bridges. Just then, the pitch on the propeller blades changed to astern and all four engines full power, the ship slowed down and came to a stop. I stopped the engines and the power came off and the ship was stopped only about 200 feet from the bridges. The third mate then picked up our anchors and we proceeded slowly through the bridges and tied up to the wall above Lock #8.

I then went down and found the chief engineer, Bill Landers. He said he knew by my frantic efforts with the engines that something was amiss. He went into the lower engineroom, where the small control box was situated. We always called this the "Brain Box", as it seemed to control everything. The chief engineer gave this brain box a kick with the side of his boot and the controls changed the propeller blades to astern pitch. I contacted the engineers at Collingwood Shipyard and told them of our troubles. They said it couldn't happen. I said it did and it nearly had two bridges knocked down. The engineer tried out his controls and said he could handle the power for the canal, so we proceeded slowly down the Welland Canal. The shipyard engineers met us in the canal and, on checking over the controls in the "brain box", found a small roller cam had worn a fibre base and had slipped to one side over the edge. They didn't make this base out of fibre anymore, but machined a new one out of aluminum and that ended that problem. The only effect it had on me was to turn my hair white!

The Fort Chambly was built for ocean-going as well as inland waters. In November of 1961, we loaded the lower holds with grain at the Lakehead for overseas; on the "tween" decks, they loaded bagged beans for England. I took the Fort Chambly as far as Montreal. All the inland crew was changed in Montreal and a salt water captain and crew took over for her first taste of salt water. She made several trips across the north Atlantic from Quebec to London, Antwerp and Le Havre, during the winter months. On the first trip over, she found the weather very bad. I am told that, for three days, the weather was so bad that the big seas tore the hatch lifter deck crane right off its moorings to the deck and landed it between the after mooring winches and deck house. It wedged itself so well that it didn't move any more and the crew were unable to go out on deck for three days.

The Fort Chambly was back in Montreal around the first week in April, 1962 and they ordered me to take over as captain again for the inland run to the Lakehead. I got inland mates and crew and we had a big job getting the ship cleaned up after her winter run on the Atlantic. We got a good break at cleaning up in Montreal. Just before we started to load package freight for the west, word came out that the Snell Lock on the Seaway would not be opened for navigation for ten days. They had some repair work that had to be done. We had a full crew aboard and expected to lay off some crew. Instead, they gave us paint and said paint out the cargo holds and "tween" deck. We painted this all aluminum and made a real good job of cleaning up the cargo space. For the 1962 season, I continued as captain of the Fort Chambly on the same run, Montreal west.

The design of the Fort York and Fort Chambly, with wheelhouse and all accomodation aft, and the power and speed you could get from these ships, made them real good weather ships. One trip I made across Lake Superior in the fall of 1958, the first season I was in the Fort York, I remember well. We left the Soo in the afternoon and proceeded across Whitefish Bay. The weather report was not good and there were a dozen ships at anchor behind Whitefish Point, on account of the weather. When I was abeam of Whitefish Point Light, the sea did not seem too bad and, as I had never had the Fort York in any bad weather, I decided to keep on going. We were doing real well and running sixteen miles an hour up as far as Caribou Island. After we passed abeam of Caribou Island Light, the seas began to get bigger. The ship was rising and falling in the head sea. I had stretched out on the settee in the back of the wheelhouse. The seas seemed to come in threes. The ship would rise on the first and come back down, then rise further on the second and still higher on the third. We were still going full speed and doing quite well when I felt the ship rise on the first sea and back down and go higher on the second and back down, then still higher on the third and, at the top of this sea, the ship hesitated and did not start back down and then went up a little higher. I came off the settee and hollered to the first mate, "Check her down". By now, the first mate started to hang on and could not reach back to the engineroom chadburn to signal the engineer to check the engine. The "York" had gone over the top of this big wave and on the way down, put the bow deck right under the blue Lake Superior water. It came over the bow and down the deck and hit the afterhouse just under the wheelhouse smashing out several windows. We kept on going right up the center of Lake Superior and put in a bad night. Our speed was reduced to six miles per hour and we were able to maintain headway at that speed. As we passed abeam of Keweenaw Peninsula, we ran into a bigger sea. It was blowing about sixty-five miles per hour. I was unable to continue on course for Passage Island and had to bring the ship around more head to, to avoid rolling too heavily. We continued on this course the rest of the night and up to about 10 o'clock in the morning. By now, we had passed to the west of Rock of Ages Light and right up to the land off Minnesota State before I could turn the ship and make a course inside of Isle Royal to get to Port Arthur, Ontario. The first mate, Carl Norton, said he never saw bigger waves in all his days as a sailor. I agreed with him, as I believe it was the biggest sea I had ever encountered, sixteen to twenty feet I'd imagine, about the height of a two-storey-house.

The Fort Chambly was also a good ship in bad weather and proved this fact on the North Atlantic run. The first season on the Fort Chambly, one trip in the fall was a good example of the sea-worthiness of this ship. We left Sault Ste. Marie on a November afternoon; the weather report was bad for Lake Superior. We proceeded across Whitefish Bay and the wind was gale force from the North-east. We were out past Parisienne Island when a friend of mine, Capt. Henry Walton, master of the U.S. Nicholson Steam Ship Company's ship, the James Watt, called me on the radio telephone. He said, "Horace, where do you think you're going with that boat? The latest weather forecast is wind at sixty-five miles per hour at Stannard Rock Light." This light is in the southern part of Lake Superior and out in the lake with nothing around it. When I answered him, I asked where he was? He said, "Anchored in Goulais Bay. We're not going out in that!" I told him I

knew the weather report was bad, but I was not going near Stannard Rock. I was going to head up to the east end of Michipicoten Island and follow the north shore of Lake Superior to the Lakehead. Capt. Walton said, "You just want to see what that new ship will do in bad weather." The Collingwood, one of my old ships, came in on radio telephone to say he was making poor time on account of the weather. He was running close under North Shore and was off Otter Head. I put the Fort Chambly on a course from Whitefish Point to pass about five miles west of Cape Gargantua. We were close enough under shore that there was no sea, but the wind was so strong, it was whipping up the water from on top of the waves and carrying it across our deck in sheets. The Fort Chambly was making real good time and not rolling at all. We caught up to the Collingwood north of the Slate Islands and passed her. The Collingwood was heading for the Lakehead too, and we were into the Lakehead hours ahead of her. We had made the trip up Lake Superior to the Lakehead with very little inconvenience.

I continued as captain of the Fort Chambly for five years and I was still in the Fort Chambly in 1967, which was to be my last season sailing the Great Lakes. The S.I.U. (Sailors' International Union) called a strike that summer. Our crew all left when we arrived in Hamilton. The ship was tied up, and the Fort St. Louis and the English River were also tied up beside the Fort Chambly. Both these ships were package freighters, and I enjoyed the company of Capt. Thiebert of Fort St. Louis and Capt. Gagne of English River. We had a real holiday taking in the Hamilton Tiger Cats football games. Each of us was doing his own cooking, as all the cooks left with the rest of the crews. Capt. Gagne was a good cook, so we had a lot of good meals on his ship. The strike was over in October and we were to get under way as soon as we got a crew aboard and our load of package freight.

My sailing career was drawing to a close, as I had only the latter part of October, November and part of December and the season would be over. I would be sixty-five years old before the next season started and I knew this would be the final wind-up of my years on the Great Lakes. I was glad the end was in sight. I was getting tired. I found out the Martian was not going to run anymore and they had no place for her captain. I called Joe Lodge, shore captain in Montreal office of Canada Steamship Lines. I told him that I would be retired before next season started and maybe he would like to keep the captain of the Martian going. As far as I was concerned, I was through anyway, if he would like to put another captain on the Fort Chambly while I was still there so he

FORT CHAMBLY loading steel at the Soo

Traditional silk hat worn at the opening of the new shed at Port Credit, Ontario

could get acquainted with the automatic controls. Lodge thought it was a good idea and sent Capt. Germain from the Fort York, as he would be the next captain of the Fort Chambly. After two trips, Capt. Germain was well acquainted with the Fort Chambly and on November 1, 1967, I left the ship in Sarnia and I have never been back.

After two years with Dominion Government and forty-four years with Canada Steamship Lines, I feel that I had a long and varied career. I had the privilege of being the captain of some of the finest ships and sailing with some fine men. With a cottage on Cameron Lake, near Tobermory, I have been putting in the summers and enjoying my retirement.

Horace and Marjorie Beaton, Great Lakes Paper Dock, Fort William, Ont.

Epilogue

Throughout the narrative, Dad rarely mentions our family, for he tends to separate family and work. In reality, we were very much a part of his life on the ships.

Our family was fortunate. Since Dad was in the passenger ships and the package freighters, we saw him briefly about every ten days. We lived in Point Edward, not far from the docks. Our lives revolved around meeting ships at all hours of the day and night. Dad would arrive home in the middle of the night with a bag full of dirty laundry and leave again the next afternoon with a bag of clean clothes.

In the earlier days, when freight handling was slower, Dad would be home at least a day and a half. Later on with the new ships, half a day was about all the time it took to unload and load again. Sometimes, the boats would by-pass "the Point" without calling for freight. Then, our family would sit in the car under the Blue Water Bridge and wait for the boat to come. When it got close enough, we would blow three long and two short blasts on the car horn. The ship's whistle would answer and Dad would come out of the wheelhouse to wave to us.

My mother rarely complained. She maintained she knew what she was doing when she married a sailor, and that he would be away from home for long periods of time. My sister and I were blithely unaware that mother must have been lonely at times. The responsibility of raising two children by herself would hardly thrill brides of today. She kept herself busy with her activities at the United Church, her bridge group and was grateful to a few good friends.

Many major decisions were made while Dad was away. Mom bought the house when he was somewhere up the lakes. Birthdays and graduations were celebrated while he was absent. I was born in September of 1935 in Owen Sound, when Dad was mate of the Renvoyle. He figured he was on Lake Superior at the time. My sister, Joan, was born in Sarnia in 1939, when Dad was first mate of the Noronic. He was home for that event, but left shortly thereafter.

In spite of the coming and going, there was no resentment by any of us. This was just part of life with a father who worked on the lakes. We were glad that we could see Dad as often as we did. Many families, whose husbands and fathers were sailors, said "good-bye" in the spring and did not welcome them home again until Christmas. In normal families, Christmas was a family time, geared to the children. For us, Christmas was a celebration of the arrival of our Dad, who now would be husband and father for three months. We went through a few weeks of what my mother called "domestication", while the captain, unused to home routine, established his land legs. When that was accomplished, the winter months were great. Mom and Dad got caught up with their socializing and we had someone to drive us to hockey games and school activities.

Then came spring. The weather did not tell us spring was here. It was my father's restlessness. He would go down to the river to check the ice conditions and to see if there were any boats moving. Anxiously, he waited for the mail from Canada Steamship Lines to confirm his appointment to another ship. Then he would pace until the phone call came with news of the starting date. Almost always, he was gone before Easter. He left in a flurry and there was a tinge of sadness, but mostly we were relieved. We knew he loved his ships and could hardly wait to get back on board, into that man's world. By the end of the winter, he had had enough of women, children and life ashore. He wanted to put the steel bows of his ship into the ice and beat somebody into port to open a new navigation season.

The highlight of my summers as a boy was the annual trip with my father. When I was about ten years old, Dad thought I was old enough to go with him by myself. That meant without my mother and sister, who always spent a week or two on board, as well.

I owe so much to those times. As soon as the ship was underway, I would go **up and stand in the bow** and look over the side. I was fascinated by the rush of the water and exhilarated by the bite of a fresh wind, feeling the throb of a great ship. They are memories I shall not forget. Neither shall I forget the "facts of life lessons" learned in the cabins of the deckhands after we had "soogeed" the decks.

The best times were at the "head of the lakes". After the ship was tied up and the unloading began, Dad and I would walk uptown and look around Port Arthur. If the boat was docked in Fort William, we would walk along the docks for miles, visiting some of his friends. Sometimes, he would borrow a car and we would go to the bush to fish for brook trout or sightsee at Kakabeka Falls. They were precious moments and made up for all the time he was away.

In June 1978, the village of Point Edward celebrated its 100th birthday. The occasion gave me an opportunity to see some old friends and visit some old haunts. Early one morning, I walked along the beach from Canatara Park to the old pier which now protects the entrance to the Sarnia Yacht Club basin. Many hours of my youth were spent swimming off that pier, which is less than half a mile from the shipping channel where the boats enter the St. Clair River. The morning was clear and calm. Lake Huron, which has always enchanted me, was blue and beautiful. I was taking it all in and recalling many memories, when the Canada Steamship Lines ship, Fort William, came out from under the Blue Water Bridge, setting her course up the channel into the open water of the lake. She is a sister ship of the Fort Chambly and looks very much like her. I could feel the vibrations of her powerful engines and listened to the whoosh of the water as she picked up speed. That ship was a special and spectacular sight. I was one with those on board. In my mind's eye, I was once again in the wheelhouse with my father, setting a new course.

C.P.B.

HAMONIC St. Clair River

1938 on board NORONIC

1945 S.S. HAMONIC

The Captain and his son. 1945, HAMONIC